Sarah Estabou

D0872191

THE TEACHERS OF GURDJIEFF

THE TEACHERS OF GURDJIEFF

by

RAFAEL LEFORT

LONDON
VICTOR GOLLANCZ LTD
1968

First published August 1966
Second impression January 1967
Third impression March 1968

575 00105 4

MADE AND PRINTED IN GREAT BRITAIN BY
THE GARDEN CITY PRESS LIMITED
LETCHWORTH, HERTFORDSHIRE

INTRODUCTION

IMMEDIATELY BEFORE THE beginning of the First
World War a man of Armenian Greek ancestry, with a
background of travel, mysticism and esoterism, arrived
back in Russia bringing a mystic teaching.

The man was George Ivanovitch Gurdjieff. His teaching was designed to permit, encourage or force man to
develop even in spite of himself.

Passing from the 'Institute for the Harmonious
Development of Man' in Tiflis, centres of study in Con-
stantinople, Berlin and London and occasional theatrical
performances of mystic dancing, he established himself,
in 1922, in the Chateau du Prieuré, at Avon near Fon-
tainebleau.

In this chateau lived, and in the case of Katherine
Mansfield died, the pupils and disciples of this man vari-
ously described as the 'twentieth century Cagliostro' and
'Master'. His methods attracted wide attention and pub-
licity, but no matter what attacks were made upon him
the 'forest philosophers', as they were called, continued
to attract more and more adherents.

There was no set 'ritual' or 'course'. Pupils were
expected to follow instructions to the letter, read deeply
of Gurdjieff's own writings and learn the complex dance

and posture 'exercises'. Gurdjieff numbered among his adherents Dr. Maurice Nicoll, who had studied under Jung, P. D. Ouspensky, Kenneth Walker, Orage, editor of the influential *New Age*, Frank Lloyd Wright and a whole host of others who lived to bless, curse or forget him.

As the teaching progressed it became more and more clear that much of Gurdjieff's philosophy was based on eastern ritual, and he himself made frequent reference to dervish practice and the names of characters familiar to students of Sufi thought. One of the most sacred pieces of music to which the 'movements' were performed was named after the Syeds or descendants of Muhammed.

In 1924 Ouspensky, who had set up groups to study what he had learned from Gurdjieff, broke with him. This break has been the cause of puzzlement and many bad guesses. However, from the sources described in this book it has been possible to obtain the true reasons for it. Gurdjieff wanted to teach Ouspensky to 'pick up' the teaching by establishing a bond between them by virtue of which the teacher could transmit to the pupil; but Ouspensky, always the correct and classic intellectual, wanted to be given the 'principles' from which to work out the most 'efficient' method. Since the system and the method of its transmission are one and the same this intellectual process had no chance of success.

Ouspensky revolted against the 'enigmatic' character of Gurdjieff's teaching. He failed to understand that Gurdjieff could only transmit his message to those who could 'decode' the enigmas. This is standard teaching practice, but Ouspensky wanted to arrive at the basis of the teaching by 'reasoning it out' and not by the traditional and most tried, most efficient, method.

Up to Gurdjieff's death in 1949, the teaching saw all manner of ups and downs; it spread to north and south America, but all the time seemed to lack something. After his death it marked time and became less positive with the mainspring gone. Was it the contact with the Source that it lacked? Be that as it may, from the 1950's onwards it carried on only because of the momentum Gurdjieff had given it. Movements, readings and lectures continued, and from time to time expeditions sought for contact with the Masters. They sought the Takamour and the Hudakar Monasteries, Yangi Hissar in Kashmir eluded them, and so did Kizil Jan in Turkestan. Perhaps if they had had the knowledge to understand that the transmission of the message is not a right but a privilege granted to those who merit it, need it and stand in the correct relation to the time element, they would have saved themselves much heart-burning. Perhaps, too, if they had had the knowledge to decode some of the names that Gurdjieff had given them they would have come up with Ashuk ul Haq, Hakim Beg, Bedar Karabeg, Bahauddin Evlia, Ahl Saz and others.

Years turned to decades, and the pupils of Gurdjieff and his successors found themselves no nearer their goal. Recognition had been withheld from those who claimed to have inherited Gurdjieff's mandate to teach. His pupils were restless, afraid of trusting their fate to those in whom they could repose little confidence. 'How can one,' they reasoned, 'trust in those who declare "When I am answering questions, I feel I should be the one asking the questions" and "To make one perfect man takes one hundred thousand years"?'

This, then, is the background against which my search began. It has ended so far as finding the Source of the teaching is concerned, yet the search to find myself has just begun, but begun with confidence, direction and discipline.

R.L.

CONTENTS

Hakim Abdul Qader drew reflectively on his water pipe, exhaled a long plume of acrid smoke and squinted at me through heavy lidded eyes before answering my question. 'Yes,' he said at length, 'yes, I knew Jurjizada, or George Gurdjieff, as you call him. He was my pupil. But why do you seek this knowledge?'

The why and wherefore were easy enough to answer. I had studied Ouspensky, Nicoll and finally Gurdjieff; I had tried to follow the meaningless pattern of repetitive activity kept up by the inheritors of Gurdjieff's mantle in Paris, and at length, disillusioned, had decided to seek the source or sources, school or teachers who had given him a glimpse of what man's destiny really is, really can be.

From crank to crank, book to book, group to group I had travelled, finding always people frozen in a pattern of thought and in a way of 'understanding' that I found to be unproductive. Did Gurdjieff, I asked myself, falsify the message, or invent it himself, or was it that the fragments of truth had not survived his death? Were his successors just trying to re-create the past and live in a sterile way because that was how they interpreted what Gurdjieff had tried to tell them?

I did not believe that Gurdjieff had made up all he

taught. I believed that somewhere there were people who had taught him, and it was they whom I sought. My aim was to find the true source of a developmental, organically harmonious activity. It was easy to be sidetracked from this by the very monolithic nature of the 'activities' in Paris and the USA, to be blinded by their claims and brainwashed by their 'movements'. True, they spoke in the name of Gurdjieff and the 'hidden masters', but could something so unproductive be valid? I thought not.

All and Everything and *Meetings With Remarkable Men* had given me distinct clues that the teaching lay in the East. I had a smattering of Persian and Turkish, and it was obvious that the continent 'As Sharq' referred to by Gurdjieff was from the Arabic As Sharq or 'The East'. Coupled with his known travels in the Near East it was obvious that this was the place to start the search. I sold up my business and left for Turkey with little idea of where to start.

Frustration! 'Do you know the name Gurdjieff or Jurjizada?'[1] Do you know anyone who knew him? Does anyone remember having heard about a man of such and such a description? No! Always no! Until Adana!

[1] 'Son of George' in Persian.

Hakim Abdul Qader

CHAPTER I

HAKIM ABDUL QADER

ADANA, IN South East Turkey, was and still is an important trade centre for goods from Syria, Lebanon, Irak and Persia. I had been referred there from Konia, centre of the Mevlavi dervishes whose patron, Jalaluddin Rumi, is buried there. The connection between Gurdjieff and the dervishes is apparent throughout his writings. Some of the movements of his dances are dervish ritual movements, while others are movements from the Moslem prayer. Konia I found to be a beautiful city, but there existed a manifest bloc between the people and myself. Although the monastic orders were suppressed in the twenties, there is a very strong 'underground' Sufi activity, and a foreigner cannot penetrate this veil.

I sought high and low, until a carpet merchant near the Tomb of Rumi advised me to go to Adana. He did not suggest any person there or any address, and may have only been trying to get rid of me, but I went nevertheless.

For several days I patrolled Adana. At long last I tackled an old weaver in the carpet serai and asked him if I could sit and watch him to learn the rudiments of his art. He demurred; Haji Abdul Qader was the master, not he. Although retired, the Haji sometimes took students.

I sought the Haji out, and after innumerable cups of

coffee broached the subject of my call and added that I was looking for traces of those men who had taught Gurdjieff. Did he know of any?

His reply made my heart skip a beat, and I hurriedly explained the reasons for my search.

'My friend,' he replied, 'I am not a Sufi in the sense in which you in the West understand the word. I am what you would call a Lay Brother, and from time to time I am sent people to teach weaving. They are sent by the head of an Order to amass a certain knowledge or technique which does not appear to have a direct relationship to esoteric study. It is not my business to enquire who my pupils are or what degree of enlightenment they have. I teach them to weave carpets and they go on their way. Gurdjieff was one of such. He stayed with me one year and a day and, though not having fully mastered the art, was sent elsewhere. He was an attentive pupil, paying more attention to the colours and patterns of the carpets than to the actual weaving, but a good pupil.'

'What did you teach him other than weaving?' I pressed.

The Haji spread his hands. 'Nothing more. I cannot teach that which I do not know. The lore of carpet weaving, the techniques and the marketing he learned from me. His inner life was not in my care but in the care of others. They said "Teach Jurjizada", and this I did.'

'Who are the "they" that sent him?' I asked, prying further.

'It is no secret,' he replied. 'The Lodge near Cape Karatas to the south. They were the disciples of Bahaddin known as the Nakshbend or Painters. They are no longer there, but in any case he must have been sent there from somewhere else because I used to go there frequently and never saw him.'

'Where would he have been sent from?'

He laughed. 'From the North or the South or the East or the West, from any of a thousand places. From another place of teaching, from another teacher. Who knows what he studied before he came to me? Perhaps falconry, music, dancing, carpentry. There is no set "course" by which you can plot a man's "career".'

'Where could the lodge have moved...?' I began, and he interrupted me.

'Lodges do not move. If they have performed their function in a specific place they are dissolved, their chief being re-assigned, if you like, and the disciples scattered to other centres. If you really want to find out who the Sheikh was I can help you. It was Mulla Ali Jamal of Kerbala in Irak. Where he is now I do not know, perhaps dead, perhaps anywhere in the world.'

I took my leave of this good man regretfully, for I would have chosen to study under him if my search had been otherwise, but now the dead trail had become alive and I must follow.

As I left my hotel en route for Diyarbekir and the Irak frontier I was handed a cryptic note by the doorman. 'Remember Abdul Qadir,' it read. Mystified, I went on my way. Certainly I would remember him, but why the note? It could mean that he wanted a reward for his information. Perhaps it meant that I should pray for him or mention his name to further contacts or...?

Baghdad is not the gem of the desert as it was described in the book of Muqadassi the Arabian geographer that I had read. Admittedly he wrote in the thirteenth century, before the advent of Genghis Khan, who paid the city a visit from which it never recovered. It has had plenty of time to recover, but seemingly lacks the energy.

The main hub is Raschid Street. Walking from the former Feisal Bridge I found, at the other end, a huge building with domes, grills and cupolas. The guide book described it as the tomb of the Sufi Saint Abdul Qadir Gilani. Abdul Qadir!—was this the Abdul Qadir I was to remember? Hastening to the Semiramis Hotel, I booked a room and engaged a guide to tour the Tomb.

No non-Moslem is allowed through the massive portals of the sanctuary, which houses tomb, mosque, school and library. According to my guide, Gilani, the founder of the Qadiri Order is venerated by all Sufis as a Great Master, and his degree of enlightenment made him a teacher of all Sufis no matter what their Order. I prowled around but could glean little. I marked down a calligrapher's shop nearby which I intended to visit the next day to buy some of the illuminated texts displayed in his window.

In the morning the shop was empty save for an urchin busy mixing inks, who spoke only Arabic. His master, he said, by dint of much pointing and waving, was in the Mosque but would be back shortly. I waited and thus found Hashim Mohamed Khattat, another teacher of Gurdjieff.

Hashim Mohamed Khattat

CHAPTER II

HASHIM MOHAMED KHATTAT

KHATTAT WAS A mild-mannered Iraki Arab whose steely gaze and erect carriage belied his four score and nine years. He greeted me with old-world courtesy and, in broken Persian, explained that the samples of Kufic calligraphy were not for sale. He would make me others and send them to me if I had not the time to wait for their completion. Talk turned to the Shrine at Kerbala where the grandson of the Prophet Muhammed is buried, and another piece clicked into place. Hussein was the name of the grandson of the Prophet and the name of the grandson in *All and Everything*. Kerbala, home of the Sheikh of the tekia or Sufi hospice at Karatas, another name!

These thoughts, one after another, left me reeling.

I asked, 'Do you know Sheikh Ali Jamal, formerly of Karatas?'

'I knew him; he is long dead. Were you his friend?'

'No, but I seek to know of one of his pupils, Gurdjieff.'

'Why do you seek this knowledge?' The familiar question.

I explained and—pause—

'I taught Jurjizada.'

'You did! Please tell me what you taught him and how and . . .'

Hashim held up his hand. 'Stay! I taught him nothing more than my poor craft. He was under the instruction of Sheikh Muslihuddin of Oudh, then settled in Baghdad. He spent his Thursday nights with the Seekers.'

'The Seekers?'

'The Seekers of the Truth, our group within the Qadiri order. Thursday nights we spend in meditation and exercise under the direction of Sheikh Qalamuddin of the Surkhani Brotherhood.'

'What more can you tell me of Gurdjieff? Where did he live and who were his companions?'

'He lodged with the widow Bint Ahmad near the small mosque. He came to me daily at the time of the dawn prayer and we would spend the day writing, cutting reed pens and mixing ink. We would, from time to time, walk in the gardens and the bazaars and listen to the story-tellers. Gurdjieff had no Arabic and little Persian. We talked little together. Sometimes we would try to discuss the Nasreddin story that our teacher had taken as his lesson the last Thursday, or perhaps the words of the zikr or repetition. He stayed a year less one week and was gone. To Turkey, it appears.' Khattat continued, 'Little more I know. I taught Gurdjieff penmanship and know little of his life here. I could have hoped for a better pupil, but he was eager and worked hard.'

'How did he come to you?'

'He was sent to me by Sheikh Muslihuddin, whom some called Saad after his great predecessor of Shiraz. He had been in Baghdad some months before he was sent to me. I used to see him visiting the libraries and listening to the public discourses on the Koran and Hadith (traditions).

He would often sketch the layout of the city, which is, of course, based on the hexagon, and more than once asked me why the tomb of Gilani is positioned as it is in relation to the whole. It was not my place or duty to enlighten him.'

'Could you have done so?' I asked.

'For what purpose save to hear the sound of my own voice? If he needed to know the reason he would be told or given enough information to be able to work it out. It was not up to me to arrogate to myself the duty of his master. I could have told him that Baghdad is built in the form of the enneagon with the Shrine as the ninth point, but apart from its informative value he could have not profited from this. It is not hidden knowledge but useless knowledge unless you have the capacity to use it. A donkey with a load of Rumi's books is worse off than an uneducated man with a will to learn and one leaf from the Mathnavi.'

'What did you think of Gurdjieff's developmental state?'

'Divining this was not my business. As I have tried to explain, I was given the task of teaching him one thing. How or if he was reacting to it more deeply was not within my competence to chart. He was following a certain definite path of instruction on which I was a mere signpost. He was eager to learn and eager to steep himself in the traditions of my art and those of the Order but how deep it went I know not. Only his teacher in the realm of interior polishing would be able to say. Do not forget, my friend, that in the realm of Sufi action there are the outer and inner activities. They may be different, but each one is important. Gurdjieff, on instructions from the Order, spent many months writing the phrase "God have Mercy". This obviously was a blend of the two, but some others are not.'

I took my leave of Khattat and wandered the streets. It was obvious that Gurdjieff had been passed from teacher to teacher, each of whom had imparted to him some of their knowledge. I was sure that his training had been to fit him for life in the world and also in the realm of man's development. But how to knit together the tangled skeins if I could only find the artisans and not the teachers? Was there anything metaphysical to be learned from these men? Should I in turn study under them? This thought I dismissed, for it was clear that without the underlying direction that a pupil received from his spiritual master there was no good in slavishly following a pattern of mundane activity.

Disconsolate, I went over in my mind all the conversations I had had, but there was no indication. Baghdad was a centre of dervish lore, even to its layout, but it seemed that I could make no breakthrough here.

Day after day I hunted for contacts, but to no avail.

Could I be admitted to a Sufi meeting? No!

How could I be admitted? By being sent by a teacher.

How could I find one? By searching.

'Where?'

'Within yourself.'

'For what?'

'For direction.'

'Could I meet a master and ask him to accept me?'

'You have already met one, Hashim Mohamed.'

'But he said he was a calligrapher.'

'Sufi masters are not necessarily mysterious figures. They do not all teach "Sufism" as you know it, and through the channels that you expect. They may live in a place and work as carpenters, motor mechanics or fishermen. They go where they are sent, and perhaps wait years before a pupil is sent to them. You have no rights on them, you cannot claim their teaching. They may not be able or permitted to teach a person of your level.'

I went back to Hashim Khattat and asked him.

'Yes,' he replied, 'I have a task here. It does not include taking on random pupils. I cannot accept you. If you want to follow the path that Gurdjieff followed out of pure curiosity or hero worship, then abandon your search, for it will profit you naught and bring you sorrow. Neither, for that matter, will following his teaching benefit you, for the Sheikh ul Mashaikh has declared that what residual baraka[1] there was in Gurdjieff's teaching left with the beginning of the last year of the first half of your twentieth century.'

'Who is the Sheikh ul Mashaikh and where...' I began.

Hashim held up his hand. 'None of these questions has an answer for you. Just because you ask means nothing! Search, but let your motive be development and attunement with the Infinite, not the aping of a teaching in a

[1] Impalpable force held to be possessed only by the great Sufi masters and imparted to people, situations, places and objects for a specific reason.

run-down and sterile form as it is expressed at present. See Ali Jamal's disciple in Kerbala, Sheikh Daud Yusuf, and now please allow me to return to my work.'

I stammered my thanks and left. I could not say that things were falling into place, but only that they were a little less obscure. I must go to Kerbala.

Sheikh Daud Yusuf

CHAPTER III

SHEIKH DAUD YUSUF

KERBALA IS NOT an easy place to stay in for it is the centre of Shiah fanaticism, and non-Moslems, in fact non-Shias, were actively discouraged from visiting this city. The sanctuary there is relatively new, as the original one was razed by an orthodox Sunni Caliph of Irak as being the focal point of a heretical belief. My welcome was not made any warmer by the fact that I let slip that I sought Sheikh Daud Yusuf, an orthodox churchman whose presence, apparently, was only tolerated in Kerbala by the Shia majority because he was so widely renowned that they could not threaten or molest him. He was not available for casual audience even though I mentioned Hashim Khattat as a reference. It appeared that had I merited his attention Hashim would have given me a key phrase to send to the Sheikh that would have assured me audience. One of his disciples, to whom I spoke, asked me repeatedly, 'What did Hashim send you with?', and again and again I had to repeat his words which, in their estimation, fell short of what was necessary.

The Sheikh's address was unobtainable, his time-table obscure and the possibilities of an audience doubtful. That I was a non-Moslem did not seem to be against me, but my being a non-dervish certainly was. I was certain

now that much of the seemingly innocuous conversations
that I had had with his disciples was staged to elicit from
me code words or Sufi reactions which would show my
bona fides and/or my level of development from an esoteric point of view. Of course I was not able to cap quota-
tions or identify phrases which must have been from the
writings of dervish masters.

Nevertheless I probed away. Who was the Sheikh ul
Mashaikh? Who was Abdullah Jamavi? Of what Order
was the Sheikh? Did he possess the powers of the Sufi
masters? To all these I received enigmatic replies. The
Sheikh ul Mashaikh stood in relationship to the Grand
Sheikh as a planet stands in relationship to the Infinite.
The Grand Sheikh was more, much more than the head
of the Sufis. Was Abdullah Jamavi one of the 'Poles' (the
poles are the four chiefs of the Sufis representing the four
quarters of the globe)? The Poles are unknown except
when they are known! Was the Grand Sheikh, then, the
Grand Master of all Orders? Yes, and the Custodian of
the Tradition. The Moslem Tradition? No, the Tradition
originally manifest through Musa, Isa and Muhammed.

Could I be received by the Sheikh Jamavi? Patience so
becomes a man that if he has conscious knowledge of its
worth he could benefit himself and others by its practice!

Nearly three weeks later, during which time I had tor-
tured myself with doubts and gone over and over such
answers as I had received and those directions which I
could identify as being such, I received a summons to
meet one of the Sheikh's disciples at the shop of Sulaiman
Turki in the cloth market.

I hurried there, to find the shop thronged with buyers

and friends. Served with green tea I sat mutely on a pile
of carpets with an outward show of patience that I had
tried to cultivate. The talk was about carpets and the
conditions of the roads and the demand for certain colours
and designs. I listened with half an ear, as a number of
the languages were incomprehensible to me, and in any
case I was awaiting some indication as to how or where I
could see the Sheikh. True, the message had contained no
such promise, but I was convinced that he would be there
some time. In this highly keyed-up state I was hardly
aware of one of the customers addressing a question to me
in Persian. I came out of my reverie to hear him repeat,
'Do you think this rug would be a good one for me to use
for my meditations?'

'Yes,' I said, 'I don't see why not.'

'You don't see why not!' came the devastating reply.
'Because you have not looked. The colours are un-
harmonious and would disturb you. The pattern runs
counter to the positive thought-stream and upsets the
tranquillity of mind. With such a primitive evaluation of
a simple thing like this you demonstrate little talent, and
yet you seek to understand things from a teacher of
Jurjizada!'

I jerked upright. 'Then you—you are Sheikh Daud.'

'I am.'

'I'm sorry, you see . . .'

'I see very plainly.'

'Well, I mean . . .'

'What do you mean?'

'I need help.'

'To what end?'

'To find myself.'

'And then what?'

'To know myself and to know if I am capable of developing.'

'To what end?'

'To be in harmony with the organic development of the cosmos.'

'You have high ideas of your place in the cosmos!'

'Sheikh, I realise I am insignificant, but unless I understand how insignificant I cannot do anything constructive about my condition.'

'How do you know this?'

'From the people who charged Gurdjieff to bring their message to the West.'

'Gurdjieff is dead.'

'But his message surely lives on through those to whom Gurdjieff passed his authority.'

'Gurdjieff passed his authority to none. His message died with him.'

'Then there is no value in what he said?'

'There was value when it was projected, in the place where it was projected. It was only one step towards a fuller realisation of the complete message. A step towards preparing a climate of a certain character. He charged none to carry the dead embers into the future under the name of a burning fire. If some did, then they show their inability to distinguish between cold embers and burning fire. Embers owe their existence to flame, and once this is gone they are inert carbon and only of use to those who use carbon and not to those who seek the warmth and energy of flame.'

'Sheikh,' I pleaded, 'may I ask you about Gurdjieff?'

'Are you concerned with the man or the teaching?'

'Both, but to a different degree.'

'Know, then, that Gurdjieff was my pupil, sent to me by my own master Abdullah Jamavi from Damascus. He came to me to learn the teachings of Salman Farsi. I taught him what his competence could comprehend, no more, no less.

'Salman Farsi was the disciple of the great teachers, and his message came through Bahaddin Nakshbend and Shah Gwath to Sheikh Abdullah Shattar. It is the rapid technique of development by means of which the pupil makes swifter progress than by ordinary methods, but which is applied only to those who have a specific reason and distinct permission from their master. This method is not always applied even when it is mastered, but for some realms of teaching it is necessary that it should be known. Gurdjieff learned it from me but did not use it in exactly the way he learned it. It possesses immense flexibility, and thus even a part of it can be used where necessary to produce an effect.'

'Would it help me to know it?' I queried hopefully.

'The question does not arise, as it will not be taught to you by me. Whether or not you are instructed in it later will depend on when or if you are ready for it, and if it is necessary then for you to learn it. Many advanced dervishes do not know it, for it has not been adjudged necessary for them to learn it.'

'What of Gurdjieff as a man?'

'A man he certainly was, with all the weaknesses and inefficiencies of the species. A developed man, no, but as

to whether he became one or not is not for me to guess.
For although I know well the history of his activities in
Europe, not much can be learned from this unless you
know the specific orders under which he was acting.'

'Who would have issued the orders?'

'The Centre.'

'Which is. . . ?'

'Do not continue to try to worm out of me information which will not benefit you. For the first time in your
life you have heard of a Centre, and now, before even
thinking over the implications of this, you want to know
where it is and by whom or what it is run. You have no
claim on my knowledge or right to an answer to every
question you can think up. Probe me less deeply for your
own sake, and you may learn more.'

'Pardon me, Sheikh, for I have travelled far and . . .'

'Travelled far!' he laughed. 'A few hundred miles and
most of that by aeroplane, and you call that far! Picking
up scraps of jumbled information like a dog scavenging in
a refuse pit, and you use this great travel as an excuse for
your lack of finesse and try to pry from me answers to
questions that do not concern you about a man whose
message is dead! I should have judged you less harshly if
you had asked if the original teaching had or would reach
the West again, instead of trying to blow on the dead
embers of the shadow of a fire.'

'May I ask you that? Where can I find the new projection?'

'You may not ask me! Your inability to ask this
question is enough proof to me that you are not ready for
the answer. You are so full of the complexities of cosmic

formulations, numbered personalities and curious deviations of Shattar, which you have learned parrot fashion, that your fragmented consciousness will not allow you to ask the right questions at the right times and profit from the answers. You have been "educated" or conditioned to think according to a pattern. This thinking is sterile.'

'How can I learn if I do not ask?'

'Your very question marks you. You learn by doing and not by asking. It is not why you should read a certain book or when or where but rather how you should read it to experience what is in it to be experienced. You have been brought up to imagine that every question has an answer. This is not true. Every question is capable of being answered, but as to whether the answer is valuable is a different matter. You feel that you must ask, have the right to ask, and have the intelligence to understand the answer, and you also, doubtless, have a university degree. Does your "intellect" help you in the realm of manual dexterity if you are clumsy? Can your dermatitis be cured more rapidly if you have a degree? Can you run a mile faster than a stupid but muscular athlete? Does your intellect lend wings to your feet? Learning, knowledge and wisdom are only useful to you if you have the companion capability of applying them in the right quality in the right context of activity.'

'May I ask, then, will it benefit me to search for the masters of a man I have never met but for whom I have a profound respect?'

'Yes, providing that this respect is a respect for the quality of his teaching and not essentially for the man himself. You can come so close to the cult of personality that you do not see the meaning behind the man. If his personality impacts upon you, search for what gave him that personality and you may taste of it too. Sanctify only the memory of a man and you sanctify a creature as frail as yourself. In January seek Qarmani in Damascus in the copper bazaar. Retreat until then to Jerusalem and think of Isa bin Yusuf. Farewell!' And he was gone.

The shop was still full of talk and people, but for me it was empty, and so was I; but I felt it to be a good emptying, like the pressure release when an abscess is lanced. I realised with a shock that I had no recollection of what the Sheikh had looked like. His voice had held me, a voice speaking Persian with the accent of Afghanistan. I tried hard to recollect any impression of his age, but nothing remained, and had it not been for the rug that lay on the floor before me I might have imagined everything.

Jerusalem, partitioned between warring Jordan and Israel, is really a city unchanged by time. I mean, of course, the Old Jerusalem, not the new city.

Time has stood still to give the narrow alleys, aged stone walls, watchtowers and buildings an air of living history. I could not help a shiver of excitement as I arrived. Here within the walls of this city some of the greatest men of history, Christian, Jew and Moslem, had lived and taught.

On Mount Moriah, near the Holy Sepulchre, stand the twin sanctuaries of Islam, the Dome of the Rock and the Mosque of Omar, companion and successor of Muhammed. There too are the last fragments of the Temple of Solomon. Hallowed by three religions, surely the city must hold something for the true seeker! Perhaps my anticipation had been heightened by the directive I had received. It was the 1st of December and so I had one month during which to study and allow the city to make its impact on me.

I knew it would work on me. I sensed that the men through whose hands Gurdjieff had passed were not given to arid whims. I felt that in this city lay a message for the real entity that was within me. That entity that had to be nourished and succoured from the chaos that surrounded it.

My search had been to follow the footsteps of a man whom I called Master. This search I would continue, but with a subtle difference. The difference was what I would try to learn, try to take in, try to be receptive. I sought a teaching to be followed within the context of the present day, not a sterile pantomime devoid of roots. The men in whom I would place my confidence were the men who had shaped him that we knew as George Gurdjieff and who had no duty to shape me.

Yet I knew that even the crumbs from their table would be particles of Truth. Particles I could use to scour the rusted and pitted surface of the interior life which I felt lay dormant within me. Scour and polish the surface so that I could see the true me in its shining form, and keep that surface shining so that no spurious reflection could bewitch me or fragment my consciousness.

Isa bin Yusuf-Jesus son of Joseph. The directive had been to think of his traditions. Where better to drink in his message than where he had lived and died?

What should be the direction of my thoughts? Was I to model them on him or form an opinion within my limitations? Should I see him as a man, a teacher, a healer, a mystic or a combination? As a complete man possessing all the faculties which I sought, but lacked to the extent that they were mere shadows to me? Should I use what literature was available or develop my own attitude? If, as one sheikh had said, a man's message dies with him, then surely the hallowed traditions enshrined in *All and Everything* or *Meetings With Remarkable Men* would not aid me.

I could not help harking back to the teaching as we knew it in Paris. Was it all sterile? Was none of it a useful basis of activity? Was it really now a mechanical repetition of doctrine and dance which had once been applicable?

I was profoundly affected by the stories of Gurdjieff's last months and his dying words. According to all evidence he seemed to lose interest during the last few months of his life. I recalled the words of Hashim Khattat that the relationship between Gurdjieff and the Masters had ended at the beginning of the last year of the first half of the twentieth century—1949, the year Gurdjieff died. Did he himself know that the connection had lapsed? That there was no point in his teaching further? He must have been fully aware that the continuation of his teaching, as his pupils knew it, would not help them, would in fact confuse them. Is that why his final words are said to have been, 'I leave you all in a fine mess'? Surely, if he had known that they were going to carry out their activities under direction from the source of the teaching, he would have exhorted them to 'Be' or 'Do' as he so often did during his lifetime. Upon anguished reflection I could not believe that Gurdjieff's message was a complete one. That he was sent to prepare an area for a certain purpose I did not doubt. Whether the 'follow up' of the main teaching was to come or had come I knew not, nor was I prepared to hazard a guess. It was quite evident to me that the inheritors of Gurdjieff's mantle in the West had taken it upon themselves to continue along the lines that he had taught. I was sure that they did this with no mandate from Gurdjieff to 'carry on', or with the further mandate of the Masters. What a fate for a message when Gurdjieff himself had railed all his life against 'mechanical thinking'!

I found myself analysing the present situation in the West. Abject fear ruled! Not discipline or respect for authority but blind, unreasoning fear. Fear of what? Fear that one of the self-elected powers-that-be would damn the person in the life hereafter? Fear that questions or opposition might be heresy? Gurdjieff insisted on unquestioning obedience and utter discipline. Discipline is the immediate reaction to a command as a result of a wish channelled into a desire and an identification, while unthinking obedience is an action produced by terror, inefficient, clumsy, dulling the reactive machinery. Development through fear? I think not, for when one's brain is frozen by fear one cannot think, act, do or be. Perhaps such a system attracts those who equate fear with authority or who need such treatment.

Gurdjieff, I suspect, used terror, but as an instrument with which he was familiar. It was not used as a way of life. What is left is a hangover of horror, indulgence and rather sickening pantomime. Gurdjieff spoke in broken phrases because of his lack of command of certain languages, but is that a metaphysical mandate for some to mimic this trait in all seriousness? Sympathetic magic? Over-identification? Or because there is nothing else to manifest?

But back to my own present problem. Shall I then search dervish literature for traditions about Jesus? Shall I see what they make of this man who himself never claimed to be a complement of God or the hypostatis of the Divinity? Shall I concur with the Council of Nice which fixed the nature of Jesus, and thus not be able to aspire myself to the completeness that was Jesus? If he was good and kind, sweet and noble, wise, frugal and full of compassion, which none will deny, this is no great surprise if he was part of the very nature and texture of God. Without being frivolous one could say that if his Divine status is true and not, as reason suggests, an old legacy bequeathed by the anthropomorphism of bygone ages, then he had a head start!

His personality is clothed in mystery and legend. What we have in the New Testament is, to be charitable, less accurate than one might hope. Matthew Arnold has advanced conclusive proofs to show the utter unreliability of New Testament records. If one accepts that the unlettered masses needed a closer contact with an All Powerful Deity than through a mystical teaching, one can appreciate that some form of teaching on a lower level was necessary, but was it necessary to promote the Messenger to partake in the texture of Divinity and thus be a concrete link between man and God? Again, if one believes, as I do, that passages unpalatable to the early fathers of the Church were cut out to strengthen their mandate as intermediaries, leaving none of the esoterica by which man could find himself and, by finding himself, find God, then the picture is very clear. Pauline Christianity, transplanted from its nursery and based upon mutilated and edited doctrine, left behind its stark realism, its esoteric teaching, and became codified rather than experimental, moulded for the new world of tottering paganism rather than being the template for a basic, direct belief by which man could find God—perhaps in spite of himself, but find Him none the less.

Moslem mystical writers call Jesus a Prophet, a Teacher, a Messenger, and give him the rank of Insan Kamil or Complete Man. Many of their historians deal with his life and teachings and dwell on the esoteric side to the exclusion of much that appears in later Gospels collected a generation after his death. Abdul Qarn of Ramallah records an occasion when Jesus and the disciples performed a 'circle dance' strikingly similar to that of the Whirling Dervishes. This appears in some of the Apocrypha, as do tales of mystical meaning. None of these mystic tales has received the cachet of Church approval, and yet they are fresh occurrences! That is to say, none of them appears in the legends that formed parts of religions or fables before Jesus' birth. From whence, then, did they come unless they had actually taken place?

Studying and wandering, I passed my time in Jerusalem. I sought no contacts, but just contented myself in preparing in the only way I knew, by meditation, for the next step. I spent much time in the public garden near the Dome of the Rock, which is built in an octagonal shape. In addition to covering the rock upon which Muhammed is said to have alighted during his famous night journey from Mecca to paradise, it is said to be the spot where Jews came once a year to anoint the stones with oil, weep and lament. Archaeologists are divided as to whether it was the original site of the Altar of the Burnt Offering.[1] From a ground plan it can be seen that the outer octagon contains yet another octagon consisting of eight pillars carrying twenty-four arches. Each segment of the outer octagon is pierced by five windows.

The peace in the garden was majestic. Tall poplars, fountains and tiles delighted the eye, while the low chant of the Koran readers became the theme music. On Thursday nights a multitude of people would descend and perform silent meditation or the more vocal recitations of dervish ritual. There was no music or clapping as I had seen in North Africa, but a measured murmur of litany and sometimes the ritual deep inhalations and exhalations which, I was told, mark a special ceremony. I could have sat there for ever tuning myself to the emanations of these pure souls, yet the urge was nagging me to seek the lessons of Jesus, though it be only (only!) to drink deep the magnetic atmosphere of this crossroad of faith.

It was not until the 18th of December that I received some indication as to what I should study. I had been consciously expecting some reading or activity while not really being aware of the atmospheric impregnation of the area. Perhaps it was the actual stay there that was to be a living study of Jesus; perhaps the daily contact with the very streets that he had walked was to be my

[1] *The Bordeaux Pilgrim (Geiger, Itinera Heirosolymitana).*

lesson. This I had begun to accept when a man whose acquaintance I had made in the Jordan Tourist Police, Mohamed Ali, who spoke English quite well, said to me in a relaxed fashion as we sat sipping coffee one evening, 'Have you read the Manichæan Gospels of Leucius, one of the Companions of John? Called, I think, the Acts of John?'

I replied that I had read the Apocrypha in my youth but only the Old Testament ones, and had not had much interest in others.

'It's interesting,' he said, 'especially concerning an event described as having taken place in Jesus' lifetime shortly before he was crucified. It concerns a dance form.'

I looked at him sharply but his face showed nothing. Was this the 'indication' that I had sought? Or was I in such a hyper-sensitive state that I was starting to read meanings into everything? Surely it was inevitable, in Jerusalem, that talk should turn to Jesus and yet . . .

That afternoon I borrowed a book which contained the Acts of John. There, from verse 94 onwards, there is an unmistakable description of a ritual dance with the disciples moving in a ring around Jesus, chanting responses. It is described that they emerged 'dazed' or in a trance state, and that Jesus appeared to John after the crucifixion and described to him certain mysteries but not in a voice known to him.

I include the passages *in toto* as I cannot do justice to what I consider to be of great importance. It does away with the theory, as far as I am concerned, that the New Testament, as we know it, is complete.

I had no doubt at all that the passages form a part of

the esoteric teachings of Christianity which were a bar to the hierophantic mandate sought by the priesthood and were cut out. How else can one explain the half-truths and seeming contradictions in the Bible?

It may be said that I was excited when I made this discovery, and that I *wanted* to believe it. This could be a valid attitude yet surely, if a man finds satisfaction in a belief that is free from the fetters of prejudice, conditioning and hierarchical monopoly, he can be said to have found faith?

The implications of the passage are electrifying. I do not seek to show that Jesus was a Sufi dervish or that the dervishes copied the teachings of Jesus. Whatever the connections, who was what or who copied whom are immaterial. Academicians may split hairs and argue about neo-Platonism, and which came first, the chicken or the egg; but as far as I am concerned I want to nourish my inner being if I still have one, no matter who first inspired belief or organised a teaching. To me this passage is adequate proof that Jesus used a technique which is identical with that used by dervishes today and similar to that used in the west by Gurdjieff. Ergo, they are valuable in 'opening' or preparing one for a heightened perception. Again and again I read the passage, and the more I read the more wonder filled me.[1]

94 Now before he was taken by the lawless Jews, who also were governed by (had their law from) the lawless serpent, he gathered all of us together and said: Before I am delivered up

[1] Acts of John, *The Apocryphal New Testament* translated by Montague Rhodes James, 1924, reprinted by courtesy of The Clarendon Press, Oxford.

unto them let us sing an hymn to the Father, and so go forth to
that which lieth before us. He bade us therefore make as it were
a ring, holding one another's hands, and himself standing in the
midst he said : Answer Amen unto me. He began, then, to sing
an hymn and to say :

> Glory be to thee, Father.
> And we, going about in a ring, answered him : Amen.
> Glory be to thee, Word : Glory be to thee, Grace. Amen.
> Glory be to thee, Spirit : Glory be to thee, Holy One :
> Glory be to thy glory. Amen.
> We praise thee, O Father; we give thanks to thee, O Light,
>   wherein darkness dwelleth not. Amen.

95 Now whereas (*or* wherefore) we give thanks, I say :

> I would be saved, and I would save. Amen.
> I would be loosed, and I would loose. Amen.
> I would be wounded, and I would wound. Amen.
> I would be born, and I would bear. Amen.
> I would eat, and I would be eaten. Amen.
> I would hear, and I would be heard. Amen.
> I would be thought, being wholly thought. Amen.
> I would be washed, and I would wash. Amen.
> Grace danceth. I would pipe; dance ye all. Amen.
> I would mourn : lament ye all. Amen.
> The number Eight (*lit*, one ogdoad) singeth praise with
>   us. Amen.
> The number Twelve danceth on high. Amen.
> The Whole on high hath part in *our* dancing. Amen.
> Whoso danceth not, knoweth not what cometh to pass.
>   Amen.
> I would flee, and I would stay. Amen.
> I would adorn, and I would be adorned. Amen.
> I would be united, and I would unite. Amen.
> A house I have not, and I have houses. Amen.
> A place I have not, and I have places. Amen.
> A temple I have not, and I have temples. Amen.
> A lamp am I to thee that beholdest me. Amen.

A mirror am I to thee that perceivest me. Amen.
A door am I to thee that knockest me. Amen.
A way am I to thee a wayfarer. [Amen.]

96 Now answer thou (*or* as thou respondest) unto my dancing.
Behold thyself in me who speak, and seeing what I do, keep
silence about my mysteries.

Thou that dancest, perceive what I do, for thine is this passion
of the manhood, which I am about to suffer. For thou couldest
not at all have understood what thou sufferest if I had not been
sent unto thee, as the word of the Father. Thou that sawest
what I suffer sawest me as suffering, and seeing it thou didst
not abide but wert wholly moved, moved to make wise.
Thou hast me as a bed, rest upon me. Who I am, thou shalt
know when I depart. What now I am seen to be, that I am not.
Thou shalt see when thou comest. If thou hadst known how
to suffer, thou wouldest have been able not to suffer. Learn
thou to suffer, and thou shalt be able not to suffer. What thou
knowest not, I myself will teach thee. Thy God am I, not the
God of the traitor. I would keep tune with holy souls. In me
know thou the word of wisdom. Again with me say thou :
Glory be to thee, Father; glory to thee, Word; glory to thee,
Holy Ghost. And if thou wouldst know concerning me, what
I was, *know that* with a word did I deceive all things and I was
no whit deceived. I have leaped : but do thou understand the
whole, and having understood it, say : Glory be to thee, Father.
Amen.

97 Thus, my beloved, having danced with us the Lord went
forth. And we as men gone astray or dazed with sleep fled
this way and that. I, then, when I saw him suffer, did not even
abide by his suffering, but fled unto the Mount of Olives, weep-
ing at that which had befallen. And when he was crucified
on the Friday, at the sixth hour of the day, darkness came upon
all the earth. And my Lord standing in the midst of the cave
and enlightening it, said : John, unto the multitude below in
Jerusalem I am being crucified and pierced with lances and

reeds, and gall and vinegar is given me to drink. But unto thee I speak, and what I speak hear thou. I put it into thy mind to come up into this mountain, that thou mightest hear those things which it behoveth a disciple to learn from his teacher and a man from his God.

98 And having thus spoken, he showed me a cross of light fixed (set up), and about the cross a great multitude, not having one form: and in it (the cross) was one form and one likeness [*so the MS.; I would read*: and therein was one form and one likeness: and in the cross another multitude, not having one form]. And the Lord himself I beheld above the cross, not having any shape, but only a voice: and a voice not such as was familiar to us, but one sweet and kind and truly of God, saying unto me: John, it is needful that one should hear these things from me, for I have need of one that will hear. This cross of light is sometimes called the (*or* a) word by me for your sakes, sometimes mind, sometimes Jesus, sometimes Christ, sometimes door, sometimes a way, sometimes bread, somctimes seed, sometimes resurrection, sometimes Son, sometimes Father, sometimes Spirit, sometimes life, sometimes truth, sometimes faith, sometimes grace. And by these names *it is called* as toward men: but that which it is in truth, as conceived of in itself and as spoken of unto you (MS. us), it is the marking-off of all things, and the firm uplifting of things fixed out of things unstable, and the harmony of wisdom, and indeed wisdom in harmony [this last clause in the MS. is joined to the next: 'and being wisdom in harmony']. There are [places] of the right hand and the left, powers *also*, authorities, lordships and demons, workings, threatenings, wraths, devils, Satan, and the lower root whence the nature of the things that come into being proceeded.

99 This cross, then, is that which fixed all things apart (*al.* joined all things unto itself) by the (*or* a) word, and separate off the things that are from those that are below (*lit.* the things from birth and below it), and then also, being one, streamed forth into all things (*or*, made all flow forth. *I suggested*: compacted all into [one]. But this is not the cross of wood which

thou wilt see when thou goest down hence: neither am I he
that is on the cross, whom now thou seest not, but only hearest
his (*or* a) voice. I was reckoned to be that which I am not, not
being what I was unto many others: but they will call me
(say of me) something else which is vile and not worthy of me.
As, then, the place of rest is neither seen nor spoken of, much
more shall I, the Lord thereof, be neither seen [nor spoken of].

100 Now the multitude of one aspect (*al.* [not] of one aspect)
that is about the cross is the lower nature: and they whom
thou seest in the cross, if they have not one form, *it is because*
not yet hath every member of him that came down been com-
prehended. But when the human nature (*or* the upper nature)
is taken up, and the race which draweth near unto me and
obeyeth my voice, he that now heareth me shall be united
therewith, and shall no more be that which now he is, but above
them, as I also now am. For so long as thou callest not thyself
mine, I am not that which I am (*or* was): but if thou hear me,
thou, hearing, shalt be as I am, and I shall be that which I was,
when I [have] thee as I am with myself. For from me thou
are that (which I am). Care not therefore for the many, and
them that are outside the mystery despise; for know thou that
I am wholly with the Father, and the Father with me.

101 Nothing, therefore, of the things which they will say of
me have I suffered: nay, that suffering also which I showed
unto thee and the rest in the dance, I will that it be called a
mystery. For what thou art, thou seest, for I showed it thee;
but what I am I alone know, and no man else. Suffer me then
to keep that which is mine, and that which is thine behold thou
through me, and behold me in truth, that I am, not what I said,
but what thou art able to know, because thou art akin *thereto*.
Thou hearest that I suffered, yet did I not suffer; that I suffered
not, yet did I suffer; that I was pierced, yet I was not smitten;
hanged, and I was not hanged; that blood flowed from me,
and it flowed not; and, in a word, what they say of me, that
befell me not, but what they say not, that did I suffer. Now
what those things are I signify unto thee, for I know that thou

wilt understand. Perceive thou therefore in me the praising (*al.* slaying *al.* rest) of the (*or* a) Word (Logos), the piercing of the Word, the blood of the word, the wound of the Word, the hanging up of the Word, the suffering of the Word, the nailing (fixing) of the Word, the death of the Word. And so speak I, separating off the manhood. Perceive thou therefore in the first place of the Word; then shalt thou perceive the Lord, and in the third place the man, and what he hath suffered.

Ataullah Qarmani

CHAPTER IV

ATAULLAH QARMANI

CHRISTMAS CAME AND went and then the New Year, and I was anxious to be off on the next stage of my journey. I took a taxi to Damascus and, having dug in at an hotel, launched out to find Ataullah Qarmani the coppersmith.

Since Damascus still retains the mediaeval guild divisions, I found the copper workers' bazaar without difficulty. Enquiries led me to a prosperous shop, hung with lace curtains bearing the legend 'Ataullah Qarmani, Fashioner of Copper, Servant of the All Highest'.

Hesitating on the doorstep I heard a voice from within the shop. 'The habit of hesitation destroys the habit of decision. Enter!'

Seated on an incongruous wicker chair was an elderly man, dressed in spotless white with a fringed Kurdish turban. He was bent over a table and scribing, with infinite care, characters on a copper disk that lay there. I stood awkwardly until he raised his head and bade me be seated. I sat with the stammered half-Persian, half-Arabic question, 'Where can I find the Master Ataullah?'

He raised his head with a frown. 'Who calls me "Master"?'

I stammered afresh, 'Sheikh Daud of Kerbala'.

'Not so,' came the reply and he bent again to his work.

I thought back quickly. Had Sheikh Daud used this term? Surely a man who taught Gurdjieff was a Master? Then the memories of the carpet incident flooded back to me, and 'No', I declared, 'it is I who used the term "Master", for you taught a man whom I would have been proud to call "Master".'

The old man rose and seated himself on a pile of skins. 'You have not the capacity to know if I am a Master or not. Do you seek to offer me blandishments, me, a man whose beard is longer than yours even though you had let it grow from infancy? Who is it you claim I taught?'

'Gurdjieff, Jurjizada from Armenia. Sheikh Daud said . . .' and I stopped, for Sheikh Daud had said no such thing. He had told me to seek out Qarmani, and I had taken it for granted that he was another of Gurdjieff's teachers. I started again. 'I seek the teachers of Gurdjieff. Perhaps you could help me if you are not one yourself.'

The old man sighed and signalled to a boy to bring coffee. 'You came here with a mind already made up, full of useless visions, and you blurt out words of little value. I did not teach Gurdjieff but was a fellow pupil of his under the tutelage of Abdul Hai Qalander, who is no longer with us, having gone to his reward these ten years. Such information as is useful to you I will give you, but cease reading into everything anyone says the meaning you seek or find convenient to accept. Gurdjieff was a pupil in this shop a lifetime ago. The Master, a Qalander of the Qadiri order, was working here as a coppersmith on the instructions of the Order. He taught us to fashion copper while he fashioned us. Gurdjieff stayed here a quarter of a year, living with the other apprentices in the

serai over the shop. He spoke no Arabic but Persian and
Turkish and his native Armenian. He had been sent here
by Muhsin Shah from Quds (Jerusalem), who in turn had
received him from the Sheikh of Haleb. He studied
copper, its nature and its uses while being introduced to
the study of himself in the same terms.'

'What was the life of a student?' I asked.

'We rose at five to wash, start the furnaces and break-
fast before the shop opened at 7. The Master would come
at 9, by which time we would have put in two hours' work
on the rough castings or the forming of trays, bowls and
vases that the skilled craftsmen would engrave and em-
bellish with silver. We studied design and engraving and
were expected to be able to draw complex patterns from
memory. After lunch we would study and work until
evening, when we would meet in the courtyard of the
Master's house with other disciples to hear him discourse
on religion, ethics or esoteric doctrine.'

'How did he teach,' I asked, 'from books or by question
and answer?'

Qarmani smiled reminiscently. 'He spoke, mostly, giving examples and telling stories and explaining the teaching behind them. He would ask one disciple or another
an impossible question and wait, patiently and courte-
ously, for the answer. He was unsparing in his criticism
of our manual and spiritual activities, but in such a way
that his criticisms encouraged us rather than leaving feelings of resentment or abject disappointment. He had a
sarcastic tongue that could flay one, but his sarcasm always held a teaching.'

'Was Gurdjieff a good pupil?' I asked.

'It was not for us to judge each other, as we could not distinguish one another's development as the Master could. I could give no judgement on that score even now, for I do not know for what purpose Gurdjieff was being trained. Manually dexterous he was and agile of mind, but whether he was bad or good for the task in front of him I could not tell.'

'How did you know he was being prepared for a task?'

'Because he bore all the signs of being in the ranks of those who are sent out to learn and be fashioned and then taught and sent out to teach, and besides, Muhsin Shah of Quds was one of the men charged with carrying out the teaching programme on non-Moslems. Charged by whom, you ask? Charged by the master of his master and then in turn by the Guardians of the Tradition.'

'How does a pupil get accepted into such a course?'

'In a number of different ways. By being in contact with the teaching and, after being approved, by being passed along or by being taken into the teaching to fulfil a certain circumstance or by needing the teaching himself and having the capacity to use it, even unconsciously, for the benefit of the community.'

'Why is it that pupils are required to learn carpet-weaving, carpentry, calligraphy, etc?'

'It is not that they are learning specific skills in order to master them. It is usually so that they learn something from each teacher and at the same time a skill which may stand them in good stead if they are sent somewhere to set up an outpost through which the Teaching goes on. The teacher transmits to the pupil the baraka he himself receives from his own master. This baraka works on the pupil according to the time, place and need and the circumstances in which he finds himself. If the baraka is to produce a specific effect on the person, then it is possible that the effect can only be created if the person is in a certain geographical region and in a certain time relationship with the teaching.'

'Do all masters go through this?'

'There are different masters charged with different activities. Their training is dependent upon the activity they will indulge in.'

'What did Gurdjieff learn from your Master?'

'You are asking me for an opinion. Opinions based on nothing are nothing. He studied a small part of Attar's *Mantiq ut Tayiur* (*Parliament of the Birds*) along with Sanai's Hadiqa ul Haqiqa which he had brought with him.'

'How were the texts studied?'

'By constant reading so that the different levels of meaning should be absorbed gradually. They were not read to be "understood" as you understand the term but to be absorbed into the very texture of your conscious being and your inner self. In the west the intellectual teaches that you must understand a thing to profit from it. Sufi lore places no reliance upon such a clumsy thing as your superficial ability. The baraka seeps in, often despite you, rather than being forced to wait upon the doorstep until your "intellect" permits it to filter through in an attenuated form.'

'Are there any specific exercises that go with this reading?'

'Sometimes. They can take the form of repetition of

phrases from the text you are studying or of phrases given to you by your master.'

'Do you remember if Gurdjieff had any?'

'I cannot say. I only know that he was given a phrase from Ghazzali to meditate upon. It was a quotation from the Prophet, "The people are dreaming, when they die they become awake". Also the section that reads, "Whoever thinks that the understanding of things divine rests upon strict proofs has in his thought narrowed down the wideness of God's mercy" (Ghazzali, *Deliverance from Error*) and as a litany the phrase "Lord, be merciful towards us". Whether there were any other exercises associated with these repetitions I cannot tell, for when a person is in an attitude of contemplation who, save the Sheikh, can tell what exercises he may be performing?'

'May I ask you if you have any idea as to why Sheikh Daud advised me to stay in Quds and study the life of Jesus? I could only be there one month and that does not seem long enough to absorb a lesson, although I did make what was for me a monumental discovery.' And I related my feelings about the Acts of John.

Qarmani heard me out with indifference. 'How do you know how long you need to work on something before you can be said to have profited? Have you in your mind reservations that tell you that knowledge requires a certain minimum time to gather? Do you measure baraka in time or depth? Do you measure weight in yards? Perhaps the time sufficed, perhaps not—you should ask Sheikh Hassan Effendi in Quds, and may love go with you,' and he bent again to his work.

Sheikh Hassan Effendi

SHEIKH HASSAN EFFENDI

BACK IN JERUSALEM I sought out my friend in the Tourist Police and asked him where I could find Sheikh Hassan.

'Every day at the Mosque of Omar and every evening at the Zawiyah Hindi near Herod's gate. But this much I tell you; he is not a man to answer a string of questions. He is a disciple of the great Muhsin Shah the inheritor of the robe of Sultan Fatih himself. Seek him out by all means but take care!'

As a non-Moslem I could not enter the Mosque of Omar, so I located the Zawiyah Hindi, which is a rest house for Indian pilgrims; all manner of people stay there for short or long periods.

I left a letter there after having explained my reasons to a very obliging Indian lady who spoke English. She assured me that the Sheikh would get the letter.

I waited several days until a messenger brought me a reply. It said in English: 'You wish to see me, but what prompts you to suppose that I want to see you?'

I had discovered by this time that this is a classic Sufi technique by which means Sufis discourage random enquiries by off-putting rudeness. I replied, 'My desire to add to my knowledge prompts me.'

Back came the reply, 'Can you use knowledge?'
I replied, 'Not yet, but I aspire to.'
The answer, 'Come to the Zawiyah at sundown.'
I went.

Hassan Effendi was sitting in the shade of an orange bush in the courtyard. A disciple sat behind him and to his left. The Sheikh was obviously a man of very advanced age, yet his face was smooth and unwrinkled, his eyes penetrating and his hands firm and rough. He wore a white Saudi robe and the pink and gold headdress of the Nakshbendi Order.

He politely enquired as to my health and fell silent.
I broached the object of my quest.

'Know, my friend,' he replied, 'that I am a teacher of my Order, not a stimulus for your imagination or an oracle for the credulous. You comb the world looking for the teachers of Jurjizada, and here sits one of them; yet it will profit you little to pose me the questions that are flooding your mind. I taught Gurdjieff to breathe. I say this and you burst into a flood of how's, why's and ifs and buts and can I teach you? The answer is, I can but I will not.'

'May I ask, Sheikh, why only breathing?'

'Only! Only! Stupid question! More stupid than to have asked why or how. Do you think that to learn to breathe correctly is easy? Does your shallow panting do more than supply your blood with the minimum amount of oxygen needed to keep that portion of your brain that you use alive? One of the functions of correct breathing is to carry the baraka to the farthest recesses of the deep consciousness. Undeveloped men try to use thought or random action to affect the consciousness. Neither of these works as the dose and the direction and the intensity are not known to them. Only to breathe! Do you know how long it takes before you can be trained to take your first *real* breath? Months, even years, and then only when you *know* what you are aiming for.

'Gurdjieff came to me with a capacity to breathe and I taught him how to do it and how to breathe with his system, his consciousness and his entire being. You breathe to sustain your level of existence. Higher man breathes to maintain the breakthrough that he has made into a superior realm of being. Your ignorance, while not surprising, terrifies me. Gurdjieff stayed with me for twenty years. Yes, twenty years! Five months in Erzurum and the remainder of the time in rapport with me wherever he was learning to use his breath. Do you know what can be carried into your consciousness by your breath? Do you know why a Sheikh will breathe on a disciple? Do you know why a Sheikh breathes into the ear of a newly born child? Of course you do not! You put it down to magic, primitive symbols representing life, but the practical reasons, the deadly serious business of nourishing the inner consciousness, passes you by. Flows over your head, bent as it is over physiology, psychology, causative phenomena, theoretic ecstasies. You blind yourself, life does not blind you. You call out in your pitiful arrogance for enlightenment, you claim your right to it as a birthright. You earn it, my friend, you earn it by dedication, toil and discipline. A hundred years must a body travel until it is seasoned. A seeker does not become a real Sufi until the very marrow of his bones has been seasoned in the oven of reality! Talk less of "only breathing" and see how pitifully unprepared you yourself are even to approach the concept of Existence! Your capacity to profit from anything is directly proportionate to the efficiency of your system.

'This is true physiologically as well as esoterically. You cannot, and you know it, expect your body to extract and process sugar if you have no pancreas, and yet, in your arrogant, intellectual way, you expect to be able to profit from the knowledge that others have bought for you. You want to use what you call the "process of thought or logic" to pick over the whole and eat the parts that you consider nourishing. At best your thought processes are surface reactions, at worst you cannot absorb a reaction or thought before it is fallen upon, diluted, dissected and malformed by the infernal process that you call academic reasoning. Reason, you call it! Do you call it reasonable to gulp down great pieces of wisdom and regurgitate them in the form of theory, the speech and the drivellings of a raw mind? The so-called Age of Reason in Europe produced less reason, less *real* intellectual progress, than one day's activity by a developed man.

'You aspire, you dream, but you do not do! Tenacity is replaced by hair-splitting, courage by bluster, and disciplined thought by narrow, pedantic attempts at reason. Bend what little you have left of your intellect to practical activity, realising your severe shortcomings. Cease your diabolic "examination of self". Who am I? How many I's do I have? You have not the capacity at all to understand the concept of true self-examination. Follow a valid philosophy or condemn yourself to join the generations who have drowned themselves in the stagnant pools of slime that they call the reservoirs of reason and intellect!

'You have no reason, no intellect, do you understand? Even less have you of the catalytic substance that would allow you to use the reason and intellect that might just have survived the conditioning you have so warmly welcomed.

'Yes, I only taught Gurdjieff to breathe! No more, no less. If you can start to have the vaguest impression of what that could really mean, then you have promise. I am not prepared to explain to you further your incapacities, brought about by your positive, negative and neuter selves and the control and effect that they have on your already fragmented consciousness. You may write a book about your search, but note me well. Quote me if you will but do not interpret me. I am speaking to you in your mother tongue so there is no room for impressions or an intellectual interpretation of what you may think I have said. If you cannot profit from it, do not try to "explain" it to others or attempt to expound your "feelings and emotions" and the attitudes that our talk has engendered in you. There are no hidden meanings in what I have said, you have all the necessary facts to assist you. Do not interpolate and do not parenthesise or stress where I have done neither.

'The curse of the western world has always been the scholar with a burning drive to interpret, comment and explain. Translation to him was a means of producing a trend of thought that had, more often than not, not existed in the original manuscript. If he, as was too often the case, did not pick up the original train of thought, he introduced his own, often deliberately, to prove a point or to use it as proof of his favourite theory.

'Due to the paucity of bi-lingual scholars in the west, these abuses went unnoticed often for centuries, sometimes for ever. Thus theories, sayings or treatises of considerable value were lost to the west. Sad? Unfair? You think so? Yet where is the blame if society has a lack of trained men? Their own or another's? To allow whole theories and traditions to be built up on the vagaries of one expert is rank irresponsibility. With your own right hand you throttle yourself while protesting that there is no one to protect you.

'Western scholarship has canonised its own saints, elevated its own self-perpetuating hierarchy of high priests, not having the critical faculty of being able to examine their qualifications. So you are stuck with them. If you overturn them now, have a pogrom and a burning of the books, with whom will you replace them? Whole schools of thought have been built on one man's aberration. You may say that that is the way scholarship operates in the West. You call it theory leading to a basis of understanding. True, yet there is dishonesty here, for why should not the translator or interpreter declare his real interest and not pass off the text as an embodiment of the real manuscript or text?

'What has this to do with Gurdjieff, you are thinking to yourself? Quite a lot.

'Those who have eyes to see, let them see the connection, those who have ears to hear, let them hear the truth from amidst the tangled skeins of falsehood, but let them first develop the faculty to know the texture of truth, to feel the truth, to speak the truth and create a climate in which truth is the accepted norm and not something out of the ordinary.

'Gurdjieff was to teach certain things for a certain circumstance. That his teaching was to be adulterated and carried out long after its effectiveness had gone, under circumstances which were in any case changed, was inevitable and predictable. His role was a preparative one, but most of the progress that was made was diluted beyond measure by the activities after his death. How, you may ask, could those who had profited continue the contact unless they were associated with the school that he had set up? Quite easily. It must have become clear as time went by that there was a lack of texture in the repetition of former activities. At that time it would have been easy to detach and follow the particles that one had absorbed.

'Activities, real activities, in the West never lost their contact, although physically they may have appeared to do so. Malformed theories held within them the seeds of their own destruction. This is an immutable law and one which is proving itself. There are activities now that take care of those to whom real reality has not lost its taste.'

'Do you mean there are activities in Europe now?'

'I mean exactly what I say. If I had meant to add "in Europe" I would have said so. I am not given to slipshod conversation. You have your national failing of trying too hard to understand things, even to the extent of introducing extraneous facts or words into a passage to clarify it for yourself. This is an abhorrent trait and I strongly advise you to eschew it. It is not difficult and does not demand heroic effort, soul-searching and heart-burning. Just do not do it. If you have any pretensions towards discipline at all use it on yourself. If you need to cajole and bribe yourself to do a thing then better not do it, because you will only not do it on sufferance. I have little or no patience with those who are basically unprepared to take themselves in hand and take a long, cold look at themselves.

'You either can or you cannot. If you cannot it generally means that you will not. If you can then why do you not do it?

'Ask me one more question, my young friend, and only one. I will answer it and then you must go and may Truth be your guide!'

'Where, Sheikh, may I take up the trail next?'

Unhesitatingly: 'Haleb, if you wish. Mohamed Mohsin the Merchant will make you welcome—Ishk Bashad,' and he was gone.

Mohamed Mohsin the Merchant

CHAPTER VI

MOHAMED MOHSIN THE MERCHANT

ILLNESS FORCED ME to stay in Jerusalem for ten days although I was anxious to be on my way to Aleppo. The complaint was the usual one suffered by travellers unused to Middle Eastern food and, since I intended to travel by land, I wanted to be quite fit before I left.

My enforced stay enabled me to read a lot. I chose for the most part Persian authors whose work I could read or where there was a good translation in English. I wanted to see if the accusations of neo-Platonism, Gnosticism and/or Shamanism levelled against the Sufis could be supported by available fact. I confess that I laboured under great disadvantages, for I was not sufficiently conversant with the great masters of Sufi thought to be able to give any sort of judgement. Should I be safe enough in arriving at a decision which satisfied me alone? What would be the difference in the impact if I should find Sufism to have been influenced by neo-Platonic thought? Yet, if their theories were valid, did it matter whence they came or did it not?

These questions vexed me, for I felt myself perilously near bringing intellectual or academic arguments to bear on the situation.

The source material which I found, with the help of a

friendly bookseller, included Al Ghazzali, Jalaluddin
Rumi and Fariduddin Attar the Chemist.

Ghazzali is widely considered in the Moslem world to
have revivified the faith, and he bears just that title. Finding doubts in his mind, he wandered for ten years until
they were resolved. His books are believed to have influenced the thoughts of both St. Francis and Thomas
Aquinas, while being one of the bases of Islamic mystical
philosophy. His *Confessions of a Troubled Believer*, translated by Watt, are moving in the extreme: 'To begin
with, what I am looking for is knowledge of what things
really are, so I must undoubtedly try to find out what
knowledge really is.'

His research was directed towards cold analysis without
unnecessary academic verbiage or intellectual vapourings.
He sought, he sifted and above all he experienced.

To quote him: 'From whence, says a doubting inner
voice, does the reliance on self-perception come? The
most powerful sense is that of sight. Yet when it looks at
the shadow on the face of a sundial it sees it standing still
and judges that there is no motion. Then by experiment
and deeper observation, after an hour, it knows that, in
fact, the shadow is moving and, moreover, it does not
move in fits and starts but gradually and steadily by in-
finitely small distances in such a way that it is never in a
state of rest. Again, it looks at the sun and sees it small
as a shilling, yet geometrical computation shows it to be
greater than the Earth in size.'

Ghazzali was inspiring reading for me, for his tussle
with his doubts and his intellect was clearly described, as
were the bases of his every decision. I could follow his

reasoning and his impeccable logic, and rejoiced at his findings. I could easily have accepted these findings without the evidence, but the detailed explanations refreshed my consciousness and enabled me to plot a simpler course through the morass of my own immature thoughts, emotions and half-formed opinions based on conditioned thinking.

Rumi the thirteenth century mystic wrote the colossal metaphysical work the *Mathnavi*, a three-volume poem which can only be fully appreciated by the most developed souls. I could not even begin to fathom the elegant allegory and deep, vibrant truth. I could only read it on the surface and try to allow its reality to filter through. I quote the story of the Greeks and the Chinese, illustrating the difference between theological and mystical thoughts:

If you desire a parable of the hidden knowledge, tell the story of the Greeks and the Chinese.
'We are better artists,' declared the Chinese.
'We have the edge on you,' countered the Greeks.
'I will put you to a test,' said the Sultan. 'Then we shall see which of you makes good your claim.'
'Assign to us one particular room and to the Greeks another,' said the Chinese.
The two rooms faced each other, door to door, the Chinese taking one and the Greeks the other. The Chinese demanded of the king a hundred colours, so the worthy monarch opened up his treasury and every morning the Chinese received of his bounty their ration of colour.
'No hues or colours are suitable for our work,' said the Greeks. 'All we require is to get rid of the rust.' And so saying they set to work polishing.
There is a way from multicolourity to colourlessness; colour is like the clouds, colourlessness is a moon. Whatever radiance

and splendour you see in the clouds, be sure that it comes from the stars, the moon and the sun.

When the Chinese had finished their work they began drumming for joy. The king came in and saw the pictures there; the moment he encountered that sight, it stole away his wits. Then he advanced towards the Greeks, who thereupon moved the intervening curtain so that the reflection of the Chinese masterpieces struck upon the walls they had scoured clean of rust. All that the king had seen in the Chinese room showed lovelier here, so that his very eyes were snatched out of their sockets.

The Greeks, my father, are the Sufis; without repetition and books and learning, yet they have scoured their breasts clear of greed and covetousness, avarice and malice. The purity of the mirror without doubt is the heart, which receives images innumerable. The reflection of every image, whether numbered or without number, shines forth forever from the heart alone, and forever every new image that enters upon the heart shows forth within it free of all imperfection. They who have burnished their hearts have escaped from scent and colour; every moment, instantly they behold beauty.

The depth of Rumi's mysticism brings a forceful portrait of an awakened man, 'beyond religion, beyond heresy, beyond atheism, beyond doubt, beyond certitude'. The last being the third stage of the three, Rumi explains. He counts them in this way: first man worships humans, stones, money or the elements, secondly he worships God, and thirdly he does not say 'I worship' or 'I do not worship'.

Rumi counsels and warns man to seek the knowledge of himself and to apply to this unrefined self a belief or a system which will lead to a fulfilment of his destiny. One of the permanent fashioners of man's consciousness is Love. To quote him, 'Mankind has an unfulfilment, a desire, and he struggles to fulfil it through all sorts of enterprises and ambitions. But it is only in Love that he can find fulfilment, yet he must not use this in a reckless way, for the fire that can warm can also burn.'

Cardinal among the tenets of the Sufi path is that ordinary man cannot himself recognise and take advantage of the shaping influences that he needs. He must, perforce, follow a teacher who knows where these influences can be found and how and to what measure they are to be used.

Rumi constantly warns against becoming attached to the externals: 'Love the pitcher less and the water more.' He stresses the experimental aspects of development and the need to work to develop the capacity for further development.

Attar the Chemist, famed for his *Parliament of the Birds*, is well in the first rank of Sufi divines. Certainly Bunyan owes *Pilgrim's Progress* to this fable in which thirty birds, led by a hoopoe, set out to find their king. After great trials and tribulations they discover the 'king' to be within themselves. 'Abandon your timidity, your self-conceit and your unbelief, for he who makes light of his own life is delivered from himself; he is delivered from good and evil in the way of his beloved.'

Such Sufi thinkers drink deep from the well-springs of truth and reflect man's thirst for union with the infinite. I found myself swept away by their penetrating insight into man's handicaps in the search for his real self. Encompassed as he is by all manner of fears, theories and conditioning, man stands naked and unprepared to face the responsibilities of his search for the unknown. True, western thought has produced such men as Kant and

Schopenhauer and mystics like Nicoll and Ouspensky, but every one has laboured under the need to present a developmental path and all have fallen short because of the intricacies and involvements of their thinking. They were themselves products of western scholasticism with its premium on pragmatic and ponderous academic thinking and polished intellectual reasoning, devoid of the penetrating insight and rapport into human problems and weaknesses that characterised the Sufi masters. It is fair to say that no western thinker has developed himself out of the world and into the infinite, yet Rumi, Attar and others not only showed the way but trod the path to 'fana' or the extinction of self with the substancé of Truth. What greater proof of the efficacy of a teaching? The mystic St. Francis, St. Teresa of Avila and St. John of the Cross all owe their inspiration to Sufi thought.

Could I, I asked myself, afford to ignore this clear indication? Certainly Gurdjieff had been trained by these people. Could I hope to take up the thread of the teaching as it was applied today? Could I afford *not* to take the chance? The decision was plain and my search was assuming a more personal form. I would follow Gurdjieff's path, but only to find the message and the form that was applicable today.

My journey to Aleppo was fraught with delays and difficulties in the shape of breakdowns, and it was not until a Friday morning that I arrived. Putting up at an hotel I asked for Mohamed Mohsin the Merchant, to find that he was, in fact, retired and lived at the village of El Bab, a few miles away. I found a young man who offered to guide me, saying that he lived in the village himself and would be glad of the lift.

Jolting down the dusty road, he spoke in terms of great reverence of the Merchant, giving him the title of Gul Bashi or Flower Tenderer. I queried the reason for this, and was told that he had always been known thus.

The village was near and teemed with life. My guide indicated a track outside the village, down which the car could not pass. This led to the Merchant's dwelling, and he suggested that we went on foot, leaving a shepherd boy to look after the car. The track was steep and dusty, in fact it was a dried-up stream-bed, and led into the foot-hills. After half-an-hour the boy pointed to a scarcely discernible house in the cleft of a hill.

'Yonder,' he said.

It took us over an hour to reach the fair-sized dwelling of stone built against the cliff face. The huge door was carved with intricate designs, and a small barred window opened to our knocking. Explaining the reason for my journey, I asked if I might see the Merchant. The face vanished, and after five minutes the door swung open and we were ushered into the inner courtyard, in which fountains played amidst gravel walks and flower beds. In one corner, near a number of rose trees, sat a wizened figure in a white and blue robe, surrounded by others in white robes. He motioned me to sit, my guide having made his farewells and gone. I sat on the smooth turf and hoped we should have a language in common. I need not have worried, for Mohsin turned again to his audience and resumed his discourse in English, accented certainly but very fluent.

'And so you can readily understand that unless the information you have is interpreted in the right way, using the right scale of measurement, you will inevitably come up with an incorrect appraisal of its character. View these matters of which I have spoken only, I repeat only, using the reference points I have given you and in no circumstances view them by emotional, social, political or other values. They may have these connections, but shun them like the very plague. Never allow yourselves to lapse into using attitudes induced within you by the circumstances or atmosphere applying at the time. Go now and meet me again next Thursday and I will tell you more.'

After they had left, kissing my host's hand, the old man turned to me. 'Sheikh Hassan is well, I am glad to know, and you seek help from me. Know that I can give you some facts and indications, but as to whether they will help you is entirely up to you and your capacity to use them.

'You wish to know about Gurdjieff. What I can tell you will help you little, but this much I will tell you, that it can form part of a picture if you can compose it. I taught Gurdjieff the science of pharmacy and pharmacology, how to plant and use plants of importance, how to extract their essences and how to use these essences. He learned this and left me after a year. Does this help you?'

I had to confess that it did not much, as far as I could see. I remembered that Gurdjieff was said to take an interest in herbs and administering them, but I could see no further.

I remember trying to work out how old Mohsin might be and failing. His features were wizened but his teeth were perfect and his eyes undimmed. His frame, slight though it was, was not stooped and his hands were steady. If he had been Gurdjieff's teacher, at what age—when? I asked the question.

'First,' he replied, 'you must not take it for granted that to teach a person one needs his physical presence. One can be taught by any number of different ways, each equally efficient, provided that the teacher and the pupil have a strong enough bond established. With that, time and distance are of no importance. Secondly, do not imagine that one year means a period of 365 consecutive days. It can be spread out over a period. You in the west demand "continuity" for study only because your minds are so inefficient that you can forget a lesson if the second does not come within a few days of the first. You are incapable of retaining all the incidents, circumstances and facts of a lesson so vividly in your minds that you can take it up after a year without hesitation. Gurdjieff received my teaching before the end of your nineteenth century, while I was in Erzurum.'

'Were you, then, teaching there?'

'I was building a garden and in that way scattering what knowledge was necessary for the needs of that time and circumstance. Do not think that the sole language of flowers is the accepted one of visual impact or the heady wine of their perfume. Flowers change their meaning and their effect depending on their position relative to each other, in what quantity they are planted, which colours are used: all these are part of the true language of flowers.'

'But what do they indicate? Can they instruct or make

any impression on a passer-by who does not know of their real meaning?'

'Their function is on several levels. Some, that you can appreciate, are patterns of differing blooms, entertaining the senses. Other effects are to produce a micro-climate in a particular place for Travellers of the Path to rest, refresh themselves or use in any of a hundred different ways. The flowers tell him who is in the area and what is his degree of initiation. The effect that they have is not restricted to those who are conscious of their meaning— some of the effect "spills over" into their consciousness and produces in them certain ideas and thoughts that are useless unless they view them in a certain context under the guidance of a teacher.'

'Did Gurdjieff learn this science too?'

'No. It was not necessary for him to know this. There is a certain brotherhood who have the responsibility of building these gardens. They do not necessarily instruct in the technique. There are those orders that work only to "launch" or to maintain the communication or to provide the "travellers" from their ranks.'

'May I ask if the Pyramids and other monuments of the Upper Nile are of the same quality?'

'You may ask because I have offered to give you a hearing, but I cannot but be aghast at yet another example of western thought. I talk of the sky and you talk of a rope.[1] What in the name of fortune do you want to do? Involve in your thoughts extraneous matters which cannot in any way give you any wisdom? If you ask

[1] A play on the similarity between two Persian words 'asman' (sky) and 'reswan' (rope).

merely to add to your incidental knowledge, then I am again distressed by your ignorant approach. If you have travelled from your home to ask about dead civilisations, this reflects little credit on your capacities for coherent thought. Do you wish to live in the past and steep yourself in the superstitions and tales of yesteryear, or do you want to profit from a living, pulsating force that irradiates the Universe? Pyramids, Sphinxes, Towers of Babel, Arches of Nineveh! Their place is not in the future, but yours is! They are exhausted artifacts. Chase them if you will, but live with the dust that they are and do not mix with the living future.

'Do you cook yesterday's potato peelings with today's potatoes? You probably do, but do not ask me to help you but partake alone of the distasteful hotch-potch. Discipline your thoughts or, if you have none, permit others to do it for you. Give up this distressing proclivity of trying to work out everything in relation to everything else. I have seen so many of you western "thinkers" that I seek refuge from your stupidities. "Who was Mary Magdalene and where does she fit in with the *Book of the Dead* and the character of Barabbas and the *Tale of Gilgimish* and Joan of Arc and the Glastonbury Thorn and Noah and the Petit Trianon and the Empire State Building and the Grand Canyon?" The answer is that many things fit in, but on a dimension that you cannot see in your present state or comprehend through your ignorant gropings. In fact you are getting further from comprehension by the very methods you use to try to put the puzzle together. Give up this preoccupation.'

Delivering himself of this broadside, he sat back.

I tried, lamely, to explain. 'You see, Gurdjieff in his book mentions the Sand Map and I wondered . . .'.

'You wondered,' he said scornfully. 'You do not wonder enough! You read, too, of wild camels and sheep and stilts and monastries and waterfalls, yet none of these engenders in you any wonder. You never imagine an allegory in them, you take them literally and you profit not at all but seize on romantic things like Sand Maps and the lure of Ancient Egypt. Why did Gurdjieff not persevere in his search in the Nile Valley? Or for the Sarmoun Brotherhood? Was he only mentioning these to give you an allegory to proceed from yourself, to encourage your silted-up minds to clear themselves of the ages of dead thought? Do you ever think of it that way?'

I spoke boldly. 'Could you then give me some explanations that might help me to understand?'

'No. Because you seek an explanation to help you and not an experience. Fundamentally you want to be given a book marked "Secrets of the Unknown and How to Know Them", which you could follow lesson by lesson and become perfect. There is no such book that you could understand; but such a book does exist, readily procurable, yet to be able to use it, to profit from it, you must be able to experience certain things that will prepare you for further understanding. These experiences have to be undergone, not just thought about or analysed. Do not now ask me for the name of the book, for you must find it yourself. My own Master Mohamed Qadir read it all his life and had not finished it by the time his mission was over. Go now and seek Qazi Haider Gul in Homs. If you have thought of the Rose enough for your state by then,

he will take you to Master Daud. Baraka Bashad!,' and I
was ushered away by a servant.

On my return to the village my car had been polished
and there was a bouquet of flowers in the hand of the
shepherd boy. He refused payment even in chocolates. He,
too, in his way was a flower-arranger, for I still have the
bouquet of dried flowers before me as I write.

My meeting with Mohamed Mohsin had followed a
pattern which I was only hazily perceiving. These Sufi
teachers were not in the least interested in disciples, or
was it that they were not interested on the disciple's
terms? Their dictum seemed to be to provoke thought and
to destroy preconceived 'knowledge'. None of them possessed the exterior characteristics that one had been led to
expect of them. There was, without a doubt, an air of
authority and wisdom about them which was accentuated
by their tranquillity an dmagnetism, but of a real and not
of the ephemeral 'celestial' character that one finds among
the descriptions in *Meetings With Remarkable Men*.

I certainly could not question their authority or the
profound truth that lay behind their statements. I knew
only too well how unprepared, despite my years of Gurd-
jieffian 'movements', I was to take advantage of what they
said. I knew I had no right to question their outspoken
criticisms of my attitudes and western intellect as a whole.
What I still sought, somewhat desperately, was the possi-
bility of being able to throw myself into this main stream
of knowledge coming from what I was sure was the source
of the teaching, be it a mysterious monastery, a cavern in
the Hindu Kush or, for that matter, a planet in Outer
Space.

Think of the Rose! I feverishly searched my books to find what this could mean. I found the rose mentioned in every poem and every work. Allegory, of course, speaking of the object of Love.

The Rose of Baghdad was the name given to Abdul Qadir Gilani, founder of the Qadiri dervish order. The word in Arabic for Rose is but a tone away from the word meaning 'repetitive exercises, repetition of the Divine Names' (WRD and WiRD). It appears that the Rose of poetry and fable is the goal of Sufi desire. They liken themselves to the nightingale, traditionally intoxicated by the Rose.

And so I determined to study Sufi literature enough at least to cull the merest suspicion of knowledge, and then I would seek out Qazi Haider Gul in Homs.

I chose the *Mathnavi* to study. Not because I had the temerity to imagine that I was in any way developed enough to understand this massive Sufi text but because it was available in a good translation and I had the Persian version with which to compare if there was any difficulty.

It would be an exaggeration to claim even to have read through it in the three months I spent on it. Its language is so superb that, in all justice, one cannot skim through it. The depth of its teaching was beyond my capability even to begin to comprehend, but suffice it to say that, making a constant and deliberate effort to rid my mind of its conditioning, I learned more in those few months than in years before. I tried to allow the *Mathnavi* to 'flow into me' and to experience it rather than 'understand' it. It is all too easy to read into it much that is subjective, and the temptation is sometimes hard to resist. However, I had set myself resolutely to the task of refusing the traps that I was setting for myself, for I knew that it was by falling into these traps time and time again that I had been marking time in my inner life for so long.

Admittedly I could blame this on the Gurdjieff work as it exists now and claim that this atrophied teaching had held me back, but since I had gone into it and stayed voluntarily, without questioning its manifest weaknesses, all the time hoping to be rewarded with a glimpse of 'reality', I must share the blame for my state. I had never, along with scores of others, thought or been allowed to think that the original teaching, in its pure form, existed elsewhere. It was, I suppose, logical to believe that the present Gurdjieff teaching was tailored for the west, and that those who had 'inherited' its direction had been confirmed in their positions by the Masters.

As I read on, I came across more and more words, phrases and stories that I could identify in Gurdjieff's books. In the past I had taken them at their face value but now I could see that, for instance, if one knows that Karatas was a dervish school it can help one to understand more. That the explanations were not given to us could mean that our leaders did not know themselves or did not see how any benefit could accrue from our knowing them. Be that as it may, I had the bit between my teeth and was going on not in fear and trembling, as in years past, in case I put a foot wrong in the Gurdjieff movements, not in a spirit of perplexity bordering on a nervous breakdown because I could not understand the lecture on 'Cosmic Hydrogen', but in a state of confidence, perhaps not so much in myself as in dervish activity.

Qazi Haider Gul

CHAPTER VII

QAZI HAIDER GUL

QAZI HAIDER GUL of Homs was a poet. He was also an Uzbek, so my Persian again filled the bill. He received me in his own home in the old city of Homs. After the usual pleasantries he asked me, 'Do you know that Pir Daud lives in Istanbul and rarely receives visitors? Is your reason for seeing him so urgent?'

I explained and his brow cleared. 'I have heard of the man called Jurjizada and understand that he was in Pir Daud's circle when he was in Mosul, but I think it unlikely that the Pir will answer any questions about him. Why should he, in any case?'

I agreed. I explained that I was trying to 'work through' the teachers of Gurdjieff in an attempt to recapture the training that had moulded Gurdjieff, and to see if I could aspire to profit too.

He nodded. 'That is of course possible, but it would simplify matters if you merely tell Pir Daud that you come from Mohamed Mohsin Kubravi and see what he says.'

Pir Daud

CHAPTER VIII

PIR DAUD

So I FLEW, with a letter of introduction from Haider Gul, to Adana and Istanbul and sought out Pir Daud. He was a huge man with a black beard lightly flecked with grey. If he had been Gurdjieff's teacher he must have been more than a hundred years old now, but he looked sixty. He received me in his chambers in the Rustum Pasha mosque and we spoke through an interpreter.

'You are a pupil of Jurjizada?'

'Yes, in the sense that I follow those who claim to have inherited his mandate to teach.'

He made a scornful gesture. 'There is no inheritance of the teacher's baraka save among Syeds, the descendants of the Prophet. Are you, then, a pupil of Gurdjieff's message?'

'I don't know,' I replied, 'since I never met him in his lifetime and cannot say what his original message was. In any case, I am disenchanted with what is going on in his name in the west and I seek the true path.'

He nodded. 'There is nothing going on save mechanical repetition. A teacher's message does not descend to his heirs, and such was the case of Gurdjieff. If you seek knowledge you must be in tune with the developmental work that takes into consideration the circumstances and the needs of the time. You may light your home with oil lamps if you wish and if you are in an area with no electricity, but when you have the opportunity of using electric current you do so and do not hanker after the traditional ways of lighting. Do you know the difference between various types of knowledge?' He suddenly shot the question at me.

'Six months ago,' I replied, 'I would have said I think so. But now the more I think the more I know that I do not. But I can learn.'

He nodded approvingly. 'Good. To know how little you know is the first step of many. For some it is the starting point for despair or self-recrimination. To have the conviction that you can learn removes it from this impasse, but discipline is necessary. Do you have this?'

'I do now, I think,' I replied. 'Even more, I know the taste of it and the difference between this and the abject fear from which I suffered in the Gurdjieff work. Terror of the "higher-ups", terror of being summoned to see one of them, terror of being thought to be backsliding. Discipline I know to be a wholehearted desire and an identification with that with which one has allied oneself. It is a condition in which one has voluntarily given away one's freedom in certain areas to those better fitted to guide one than one is oneself.'

He looked at me fixedly. 'Is that reply from the heart or the head? By rote to please or from the heart and felt?'

I did not have to think long. 'From the heart, and deeper.'

'Good. Discipline you need to follow a hard path. Discipline to stop you from having to pause and try to think

out your next action. Discipline to overcome what you
find contradictory, irrational or confusing. You can afford
to suppress your much vaunted "critical faculty" when
you are receiving instruction from someone who really
knows what he is doing and to whom only what he is
teaching is important.

'No one not fully trained to teach may use these techniques, for fear that he will even further confuse the
already sufficiently confused intelligent mind. Techniques
have been developed over the centuries with time, place
and circumstance taken into consideration. Each activity
or technique is applied by the person in charge of an area
of activity according to the time and the need. These may
constantly change, and thus the director of the activity
must be constantly in touch with the main plan of activity.
Only activity that is carried out in step with the main plan
is valid activity. Haphazard application of half-heard or
semi-understood truths can lead to nothing except confusion, loss of time and sometimes actually retrograde
movement. Do you know what it is to be in the world and
yet not of the world?'

'I have heard of the concept but would value your
explanation.'

'It means that you must live in the world, not abandon
it like a monk or a hermit. True, at certain times according to your capacities you may be required to spend a
certain time in a place or with a brotherhood, but only
for a limited period. You must use every means to try to
excel at your job or your business, allowing techniques to
effect a change of thinking in respect to worldly activities.

'Far too many westerners seem to equate metaphysical

progress with withdrawal from the contamination of the world. You need not be contaminated by the world provided you adhere to certain basic values and beliefs. You can associate with the most terrible and depraved people and be exposed to all influences and not suffer.

'You have a place in your family and in society which you cannot escape in order to sit in a cave and meditate. You have responsibilities which you cannot slough off. Meditation, after all, can occupy twenty-five seconds as well as twenty-five years. If your system is so ineffective and inefficient that you have to meditate for twenty-five years, then something is very wrong with you or the system or perhaps both.

'If you are enlightened enough to know upon what to meditate, then you can focus certain of your mind centres upon this and meditate for a matter of seconds to the total exclusion of everything else. Sitting in a cave dressed in rags, eating nuts and berries, can only produce physiological changes or effects and precious little of an esoteric character.'

'May I ask then,' I interrupted, 'the purpose of the monastic brotherhoods of the Hindu Kush?'

'Your question is not only untimely but inaccurate,' he snapped. 'The existence of certain power houses does not change anything of what I have said. The people in those centres are concerned with the destiny of the world, but you, you cannot even begin to comprehend anything of their activities. They are no ordinary men, let alone monks. They know neither rest nor even satisfaction, for they have to make up for the shortcomings of humanity. They are the Real people who have experienced being and non-being and have long ago entered a stage of evolution when neither state means anything to them.'

'Gurdjieff said that he had visited one and that his friend Prince Lubovedski was one of the inmates. Was he one of the Immortals?'

Pir Daud's eyes flashed. 'Your unspeakable naïveté belies your years! Gurdjieff said this, Gurdjieff said that. Kant said this, Chekov said that! Everybody has something to say and you can, and sometimes do, spend your entire life reading them and painfully trying to reason this and that out and then to apply personal experiences or muddle through the results of other's experiences. It results in nothing.

'You should by now have understood that much of what Gurdjieff wrote was allegory—his characters, locations and situations. What does it mean to you even if there had existed such a Prince? And if he was one of the Abdals? You are scrabbling about in the sand, attracted by pieces of mica to knit together and make a window, not realising that the sand itself is capable of being transformed into the purest glass.

'Do not concern yourself with personalities, or with events that happened in a time sphere not relative to your present situation and not capable of being understood or applied now. Certain literature is based on experience and activities in the past and lives only during the lifetime of the teacher whose duty it was to produce a certain impact upon a limited segment of humanity.

'Ask yourself how, then, this information can have any developmental validity when the circumstances, time and people involved are no longer the same. You delude yourself in giving such matters any importance and you delude others by your popularising of it. You cannot seek refuge in the plaint "It was all that there was available" or "There was no other source". There was always a literature of action and there were always indications as to where the source could be met.

'There was never a vacuum in the projection of the teaching. It was in western thought and intellect that the vacuum existed. The west encouraged and popularised the cult of the semi-literate gurus whose sole claim to fame was a seat under a peepul tree and a yen to use the navel as a sort of anatomical crystal ball. Oh yes, the west has ever sought the "wisdom of the east", but never in the right places. Always the colourful, the faintly erotic, but never the hard reality. Western thought never recovered from the dead hand of the organised church although it had aided and abetted the monopoly of that church by never challenging its right. Any hint that the organised church did not contain the esoteric content one might have hoped for was met with the stake. I am as much a Christian as was Jesus, but I am not the type of Christian you find in the present-day fathers of the established church. Your own St. Augustine himself stated that the Christian religion existed among the ancients but he, for all his sanctity and sincerity, is held to have been influenced by unChristian teachings.

'Now you have come to the point,' he continued, 'where, encouraged by the image of a man, you want to follow his teachings. Very laudable, yet since these teachings, unlike the basis from which they spring, are no longer operative you must seek the way in which they are being projected today. When you have found this, then follow it—do not waste time in idle speculation as to how it fits with Gurdjieff or Simon Peter or Pharoah! Do you want to follow a teaching which is developed and organically in tune or do you want to piece together the relationship between one thousand and one dissimilar yet exciting circumstances, activities, people or civilisations? If the latter, then study archaeology, anthropology or cultural patterns and be satisfied with interesting finds and exciting prospects. Do you want ghostly "guides" in the shape of Red Indian chiefs and a supernatural voice speaking to you? Take up spiritualism. But if you want real progress with disciplined hard work, then get out of your pattern thinking and overweening pride and confidence in the breadth of your "intellect", and experience that which can only be experienced.

'Go now to Tabriz and there find Daggash Rustam, master of the Drum. He may see you or not. If he does, you can hope to work on. If he does not—' He spread his palms expressively.

This is not a travel book, and though the trip to Tabriz was not without interest I had a mission and it was not to see sights. Suffice it to say that one would not have made the trip without a compelling reason!

Daggash Rustam

followed.

TABRIZ, FROM WHICH the mysterious dervish teacher
Shams i Tabriz took his name, is not an impressive city.
Nervous as I was, I found the people less helpful and
sympathetic than I had hoped. Everyone knew the Master
Drummer but no one could say where I could find him.

Ten days I spent in searching until one day, as I sat in
a chai khana, my attention was drawn to a tall figure,
heavily bearded, dressed in a ragged, patched robe, crossing the street. On reaching a small open space he produced a drum and started to beat it crying, 'Hearken ye
all to Rustam'.

I jumped up, spilt my tea and rushed over.

The dervish was seated on a stone and round him a
crowd had gathered. He held up his stick for silence.

'I will tell you a tale, though why I waste my time on
you dolts I don't know,' he began. An appreciative
murmur showed that this was a known gambit.

He told the story of the dervish from Saadi's *Gulistan*
with great detail and mimicking the different voices. He
was a master storyteller indeed. Spellbound, the crowd
followed his every gesture and tone and broke into a crash
of applause as he ended his tale. Collecting a small hand-
ful of copper coins, without thanks, he strode off, followed

by a motley crowd of urchins who apparently knew that
he would buy sugar cakes at a nearby shop and distribute
them to the children. Having done this he made off. I
followed.

On the outskirts of town he forsook the road and,
beckoning me to follow, crossed a field and took his seat
on a rock by a stream. He motioned me to sit down and
gazed reflectively into the water. Once I broke the silence
but he motioned me to be quiet. After half an hour he
spoke . . .

'Ishk bashad.'

'Ishk,' I replied.

Then, 'If thou possessest knowledge, serve like those
who are ignorant; for it is unseemly that people from China
should make the pilgrimage and the native of Mecca
should lie sleeping nearby. What do you seek from me?'

'Knowledge,' I replied, 'knowledge to enable me to
think through the complexities of modern life and to
retain a firm grip on the principles of the great teachers.'

He prodded the earth with his stick. 'Such knowledge
as you seek comes from experience and cannot be learned
from a book. You can read the great ones, Rumi, Jami,
Hafiz, Saadi, but their writings are only the salt of the
bread. To taste the loaf you must eat the loaf, to experience the salt in its intimate relationship with the flour, the
yeast and the water. Your relationship with present-day
life you view on the basis of your conditioned background
and what you have been taught to think.

'To clear your palate to allow a capacity for fresh
taste you have to leave the old formulae which have let
you down so violently in the past, and seek the real values.

Are you prepared to leave the world as you know it and live in a mountain retreat on a very basic diet?'

I signified that I was.

'You see,' he nodded his head regretfully, 'you still feel that to find knowledge you must seek a solitary life away from impure things. This is a primitive attitude and one satisfactory for savages. Do you not realise that a sophisticated path of development keeps pace with the requirements of the present day? Can you comprehend the uselessness of abandoning the world for the sake of your selfish development?

'You may need a course,' he went on, 'at a Sarmoun centre, but that will not mean total abandonment of your mundane activities. There is nothing "impure" about reasonable worldly activity provided you do not allow it, nay invite it, to corrupt you. If you have enough skill you can actually harness the negative forces to serve you . . . but you must have enough skill.

'From the beginning of time our people have spoken the language of the people and have moved according to the time state of the planet. We are abreast of time and even ahead of it—not for us the sordid vestiges of an ancient teaching projected ineffectually into the twentieth century. On the contrary we are men of every century, including the twenty-first. You have read widely on oriental lore? What do you know about the impact of our music on the west?'

I replied that I knew little other than that the waltz and some Morris dancing had Sufi roots.

'True, true,' he replied, 'but apart from the actual rhythms, what of western composers who have been influenced and through whom our melodies have influenced the west? Men have taken music westwards since the ninth century as minstrels, troubadours, and bards to make an impact on western thought. Just as they did so for the lyre and the flute, so do they now for modern instruments.

'Do you know of the builders of the Middle Ages in Europe? The men whose abbeys, cathedrals and castles still stand. Do you know of the gardens that still retain the power they were made to hold and scatter in the west?

'These are only fragments of the whole vast picture. Can you reconcile this with toothless old men sitting in insanitary caves in the mountains? Do you believe that the destiny of the world can be affected by men whose only techniques and claims to fame are isolation from worldly temptation? A huge American industrial company with a sprawling network of communications, controls and agents does not exist to market one limited product. Should we who deal with life itself have less?

'Do you deliberately seek to do us an injustice? What do you know of the men whose duty it is to benefit your miserable skins in the west? Can you comprehend for one instant the immensity of the burden, waking and sleeping? The magnitude of the burden they carry for you?'

I replied that I was beginning to become aware of a fragment of the picture and that it filled me with awe and respect, but my lack of breadth of vision was born not of injustice but of ignorance, of which I was only now becoming aware. I added that I had come to Tabriz in continuation of my search for Gurdjieff's teachers but I found that my attitude was becoming more personal.

'Jurjizada,' he said, 'yes, a pupil of my own master Sheikh Durgui, under whom I studied music by order of Sheikh Yussuf of Cairo. I was a young pupil when Gurdjieff came and learned the music and the dances of the Mevlavi. I remember him quite well and his companion Dagan Muslimov of Bokhara. He stayed in the takkia with us, it was part of our duties to light the fires and sweep out the takkia. He stayed but a short time and then went back to Cairo.'

'Was Sheikh Yussuf a Mevlavi?' I asked.

'No, he was a Nakshbendi but of exalted rank, and therefore a master of the secrets of all the Orders. Such a mâster could send a pupil to any particular takkia or to any order to learn a specific part of the teaching which he would use or teach with. In Gurdjieff's case I expect he was to use some aspects of the Mevlavi music and dance in another teaching sphere. His companion was with us longer and then returned to Cairo and died, so I heard, of thirst in the desert because he had not taken enough water with him. Gurdjieff and some others were in the same party but were separated by a simoon (a sand storm). But you, where do you go now?'

I replied frankly, 'Wherever you advise me to go. I do not know how much time I have left, but I should like to use it to benefit my inner consciousness.'

He pondered. Then, 'Sheikh Abdul Muhi is in Cairo at Al Azhar. See him. We shall meet again, but go now to Cairo.'

Sheikh Abdul Muhi

CHAPTER X

SHEIKH ABDUL MUHI

THE PROFESSOR'S QUARTERS in Azhar were almost as severe as those of the students, except that they were book-lined and away from the noise and bustle outside the walls. Sheikh Abdul Muhi had welcomed me and we sat in his cubicle drinking aromatic coffee. He was a youngish man in the severe habit of an Azhar Sheikh. We spoke in French.

'Sheikh Yussuf, my teacher, is long dead. He was my father as well as my guide, and from him I learned all that I know. He was the Sheikh of the Nakshbendi Order in the Nile Valley, trained at Kizil Jan in Turkestan, and was a man of profound greatness and knowledge, un-matched patience and tenderness. I remember the inci-dent you mention concerning Gurdjieff. They were travel-ling from Omdurman to Aswan, returning from a visit to the Mahdi people, when a sand storm separated them. Muslimov did not have enough water and, during the several days of the storm, lost his camel and perished. The sheikh ordered his body to be returned to his family for burial and forbad anyone to venture into the desert with-out sufficient food and properly trained camels.'

'Was his education with your father to do with music?' I asked.

'No, he was studying certain exercises and techniques. He studied music in Tabriz after he had finished here and then returned here briefly to be examined by one of the Akldans who had been sent from Jeddah. Here, as I recall, he mastered the "stop" exercise and the "habs i dum" or breathing technique that goes with it.[1] There were also some Indian faqirs who were learning breathing techniques.'

'Is it true,' I asked, 'that the word "faqir" is of some power in itself?'

'"Faqir" comes from the Arabic root *Fuqr* which means "poverty". These men were so called as they had eschewed worldly wealth and lived by the saying of Muhammed the Prophet, "Poverty is my glory".'

'Would it,' I questioned, 'be useful to follow the exercises that Gurdjieff followed?'

'No, those specific ones were for a particular time and certain specific conditions. You have to follow ones that are distinctly constructed for your needs and the circumstances prevailing. These have to be given to you by a teaching master otherwise they are of no benefit at all.'

'How do I get these?'

'You do not "get" them! You earn them or you merit them. They are given to you by a teaching master after you have worked under him for long enough for him to see that you can benefit by them. This you show by having absorbed in the right way the teaching and by manifesting the signs, which he can identify, that you have profited to

[1] Cf. account of the stop exercise given in *Meetings with Remarkable Men* and an account in *The Sufis* by I. Shah.

the extent that you can now start to develop yourself. You start by mastering the ability to learn.

'At the moment your thinking is crude and unrefined. You have to filter a thought through a mass of unrelated and unnecessary information which you consider to be knowledge. This information has been piling up in your mind since childhood. You have remembered it because you have equated it with knowledge, but it is only facts and figures and echoes of matters that are considered to be of importance; facts and matters sanctified by conditioned thought in a conditioned society. You believe yourself to have inherited the knowledge of the ages and to have the capacity of thinking for yourself.

'What you are doing in reality is sifting through this conditioning and selecting something that you think can be usefully applied to a particular situation. The choice is usually a random one and based upon emotion rather than positive need or real knowledge. So you go on building whole sections of your reactive personality and thought on what is often, far too often, false premise, weak, inefficient and dangerous.'

'What can one do to get away from this pattern?'

'Think as you can be taught to think, using only the anchor points that are given to you to hold fast to and to navigate by. Only by a directed process can you properly use your thought capacities to their fullest advantage. Under any other process you are merely reacting and not really developing the capacity to think. This does not mean that you have to react and think in a guided way under every possible circumstance, no matter how minor, as this would produce chaos in your everyday life.

Increased thought capacity is reflected throughout the entire organism by automatic reaction in every circumstance.

'Whether one is actually conscious of the fact that one has thought out one's reaction, one in fact has, and if one is thinking according to the right rules then the reaction will be right. If the reaction is merely a surface one, it will be no deeper than a reflex. If it penetrates deeper into the murky pool of a normal person's mind consciousness —composed as it is of distractions, confusion, fear and uncertainty—then it will provoke a reaction of the same texture as that from which it was "bounced", or what was available to be selected. Obviously, insufficient evidence, incomplete learning and an inefficient thought process will produce reactions mirroring just these things.

'You think at the moment that you are thinking, but you are not using one-fifth of your real thought potential. In order to profit from thought you must know how to think and what to think and not delude yourself that your intellectual exercises are real thoughts. They are, in fact, a disgusting travesty of true thought that intoxicates and seduces but produces naught but an impairment of true thought capacity. Each time you accept one of these "shadow thoughts" you are encouraging your consciousness to accept them as real, and thus slowly undermining the value of true thought.'

'Does one,' I asked, 'still retain creative freedom of thought despite the creation of this "new pattern" thinking?'

'Your lack of grasp surprises me,' retorted the Sheikh. 'You yearn for what you term creative thought, but it is this very "creative freedom" that has let you down all these years. Creative thought, creative art or creative poetry are all excuses to expose the world to aberrations born in the sullied minds of the so-called intellectual élite of the west. The true creative artist never cries his creativeness to the skies. The true intellectual never claims to be one. It is the unfulfilled, the unsuccessful, the lazy and the foolish who weld together old bicycles and claim to be creative. They are surrounded by their own kind who shower the rubbish with praises so that, in their turn, they will be the recipients of praise.

'Measured against accepted yardsticks of art—colour, form, perception and depth—they have nothing. They cry discrimination and blame "outmoded concepts" and jealousy for the lack of respect shown to their creations by the vast majority of the human race. They claim to be a new wave of thought, a revolt against the stagnant past. Excellent! No one can be expected to laud that which, by common consent, has passed into obsolescence. But a valid thing seldom does. If a thought or an idea is basically sound, then it will develop. The so-called outmoded conventions that the wide-eyed adolescent minds in the west seek to overturn have been arrived at over the centuries. They are not restrictive in character, for no set of conventions can smother something of value. If the conventions demand some skill in art or writing or some capability in these fields, then judge for yourself the characters of those who wish to have these conventions set aside.

'In the west of today you have scarcely any original or creative thoughts or thinkers. You revolt against this statement, as a good conditioned western intellectual should,

but it is a fact. The west is undergoing a period of agonis-
ing self-examination of its values and its beliefs. To seek
God or Mammon? Where and how to seek God? What is
man's place in the Universe? None of these questions can
be answered by a society that hangs on to the every word
of the so-called, self-perpetuating thinkers of today. Their
outpourings are an affront to generations of western
thought.

'Had the centuries of western thought been properly
orientated, then it must have borne fruit on an esoteric
level, yet it has not done so even on an exoteric one. Mark
you, western man knows his limitations and flocks to the
platform of anyone claiming a new way of thought, especially from the orient. People were intoxicated by some
aspects of the teachings of Gurdjieff because to them he
represented a way of being able to get out of the trap into
which they had been led by their conditioning. They saw
in him a man who could help them recapture the old
values which they felt were a legacy for them to claim but
to which they had no access because of the morass of
intellectual theory generated by their intellectual leaders.

'Go, my friend, seek your goal by sifting the pure from
the false and seize hold of that which has survived the
centuries and emerged progressive and intact, not as a
hoary belief to be venerated but as a positive path of
action and reaction. This path does exist, it exists every-
where and in every age, yet it hides itself from the un-
ready, the sensation-seekers and the self-indulgent. It is a
hard path and one of total commitment and absolute discipline. Its reward is extinction. You recoil at this?
Perhaps you do not want to lose your "identity", that

chimera which means so much to western man? You have no identity! You are a faceless wanderer through the corridors of time, with no intrinsic value and no right to progress merely because of the accident of your birth. You earn your place in the sun or forever sit in the shadow of your "identity"! Know yourself by dedication, and when you have done that you can and will absorb yourself gladly into the matrix of truth.

'Go to Sheikh Shah Naz in Konia at the Turbe. He is the eldest pupil of the Qutub (Pillar) who directed the studies of Gurdjieff. He may see you.'

All the way to Istanbul I pondered. So categorically critical had all the sheikhs been that I wondered if I could ever shed myself of my western conditioning and try to learn anew. I thought that I might be able to, for I had caught a glimpse of the pristine truth that lay behind their discourses. I would follow, I vowed, as far as I could.

Sheikh Shah Naz

CHAPTER XI

SHEIKH SHAH NAZ

K ONIA, WHERE RUMI lived, preached and is buried, revolves around his tomb. The Sheikh was there, saying his evening prayer, after which he agreed to see me. A young boy acted as interpreter.

We met in his simple quarters behind the tomb. The room was furnished with worn carpets, and the Sheikh, in a white robe with a black hood, sign of a Sheikh of the Mevlavi Order, sat on a white sheepskin on a low couch. In front of him, on a table, lay a greenish marble star with twelve points. I had been studying Sufi ritual and I knew that this star stone—known as the Taslim Taj—is often used to show the presence of the High Sheikh of the Mevlavi Order; and my eye caught another robe, white with a blue lined hood. So the High Sheikh was in Konia.

'Can you help me with my search?' I had asked the Sheikh on entry.

He had smiled. 'My son, you see before you a man of more than eighty summers whose own search is but half over, but ask and I will try to advise you.'

'I am looking for the men who taught Gurdjieff, and seek to be accepted as a pupil,' I said boldly. 'I do not know if I am fit to be one, but I know I want to try.'

The Sheikh looked at me with penetrating blue eyes for several seconds. 'You have studied Jurjizada's writings?' 'Yes.'

'Have you learned from them?'

'I do not think so. I have a feeling that too much is hidden and that I have no means of penetrating their secret.'

'Allegory they are certainly,' he spoke slowly. 'You cannot penetrate them, for they are for another time.'

'How . . . ?' I began.

He interrupted me. 'Come,' he said and, rising, motioned me to follow him.

We walked along a passage and down some stone steps into a large chamber which I imagined lay under the main tomb. It was an octagonal shaped room some twenty feet high, and vaulted. As I looked round my gaze fell on something that made my heart miss a beat and I felt near to suffocation. It was a tall ivory post with articulated arms of the same material. Each arm was held by a man dressed in flowing white dervish robes and conical cap. They stood in different attitudes, all stock still. Seated a little way apart sat a figure on a white sheepskin, dressed in a cloak of multi-hued patches over a white robe with blue-lined hood. On his head a many-hued turban was loosely wound round a conical cap of striking hues. On his left shoulder he wore a curious three tongued buckle, of silver mesh mounted with small turquoises, and in his hand he carried a string of ivory prayer beads. His face was hidden by the shadow of his hood. I stood spellbound, drinking in the scene, until the Sheikh tugged my sleeve and we left.

Back in the sitting-room he asked me, 'What did you see?'

I replied that it was surely a meeting of dervishes, and that the 'tree' must be the one that Gurdjieff had described.

'Do you know what it was?' he asked.

I confessed ignorance.

'It was an apparatus for communication, teaching and measuring. The men holding the arms were in deep communion with the master, and in a state of "stop". Through this he can teach them on the deepest level and gauge their reactions. In every major teaching centre there is one. He communicates through this to us.'

'May I ask who he was and why you showed this to me?'

'He was one of the Qutubs and they of the Abdals. What lesson you should learn from this I leave to you.'

'Was he one of the teachers of Gurdjieff?'

'Gurdjieff never saw him.'

'Did Gurdjieff see the "tree"?'

'No, it is never used in the way he described it.'

'Can you tell me if I stand any chance of being accepted as a pupil in any school?'

'Understand that we do not recruit,' responded the old man. 'We select or we reject. Tonight you will sit with some of our friends, and tomorrow you will leave for Meshed where you will describe your experiences this night to Hassan Kerbali and he will answer your question. Go with our friend and leave early in the morning.'

Later in the evening, after supper, I was conducted to a chamber where perhaps a dozen men sat. They were dressed in western costume and sat on small carpets, each wearing a white skull cap embroidered with white silk. I was given a cap and motioned to sit in a vacant place in the circle.

After some minutes a drum began to beat and the plaintive notes of a flute invaded the stillness. Trying to think of nothing I closed my eyes and let the music enter into me. The music and the insistent beat of the drum had a hypnotic effect upon me, and I seemed to be drifting in space towards a bright star emitting rays of different colours. The soft murmured chant of Hu, Hu came into my consciousness and I joined in because I wanted to rather than because I thought I should.

A few minutes passed, the star grew brighter, and over the music and the chant I heard a voice intoning in Persian. I had read the phrase over and over again and I knew it, the opening verse of Rumi's *Mathnavi*, 'Bisnev zi nay chun hikayat mikunad' (Listen to the tale of the reed). Over and over again the voice spoke the same sentence and then I drifted back to earth and the star diminished in brilliance. It was morning.

My journey to Meshed made little impression on me. My mind was too full. My 'few minutes' of meditation had been in reality several hours. Was this hypnotism? Yet why should it be? What would be the value? The questions chased themselves round in my brain. Then I relaxed; my mission was to remember and report, not examine subjectively.

Hassan Kerbali

CHAPTER XII

HASSAN KERBALI

HASSAN KERBALI WAS an enameller in the Tilla Shahi Bazaar in Meshed. I spoke of my experience and he listened gravely. When I had finished he looked up.

'These words are your passport. Different members of that group heard different words according to their capacity to understand them. You must start at the bottom, without haste and without impatience. You must listen to the tale of the reed. If you can do this and not look back, if you can commit yourself completely, you can work towards understanding. If you allow into your raw and awakening consciousness old ideas and intellectual pleasantries, you will forfeit what foothold you have in reality.'

'I am ready to try,' I rejoined. 'I hope I have the courage to do this because I am so much a creature of my conditioning.'

'Do not use worldly conditioning,' came the gentle reproof, 'as a constantly recurring excuse. Much of the blame is your very own. You could have rejected much that you accepted uncritically.

'Man is basically greedy, lazy, and self-indulgent and seeks every opportunity to avoid tasks that need effort. Physical effort is less difficult than mental effort, and effort on a developmental level more difficult still. Mental discipline is a product of determined discipline. It is no accident that some have it and some not. If you are prepared to struggle with yourself, good; otherwise seek an easier way, which will lead you nowhere but give you an idea that life's mysteries are open to you.

'Pick Zen, Theosophy or Yoga, are all refuges for the incapable who want something to occupy their time and give them something both supernatural and seemingly rewarding to hold on to. If they would but use in directing their mental processes one quarter of the energy they use tying themselves in knots and in other curious activities, they would proceed further.

'Go now to Sheikh Mohamed Daud in Qandahar. Tell him that Hassan Chainaki greets him.' And he turned again to his work.

Crossing the Afghan frontier I felt that real progress had been made. Gurdjieff had mentioned Afghanistan and Bokhara and the Amu Darya and the Hindu Kush and Karffiristan in his writings as being of vital importance, and I felt that I was on the homeground of the tradition.

Sheikh Mohamed Daud

CHAPTER XIII

SHEIKH MOHAMED DAUD

QANDAHAR WAS HOT, dusty and hospitable. Sheikh Daud had a tea-house near the Shrine of the Prophet's cloak and greeted me cordially, making arrangements for me to stay with his son. I gave him the message from Meshed and his bearded face grew serious.

'Brother,' he said gravely, 'know that the path you have chosen is long and arduous. Nothing save full submission to your teacher will carry you through the difficulties that you will meet. Complete and unswerving belief and trust in him are your only guidelines. Any hesitation or negative response will not only disturb, they will produce doubts and errors which will cloud your understanding.'

'Forget now about Gurdjieff. That teaching is not for you. What is now outmoded will gain you nothing. A teaching that is designed to be transmitted at a specific time lasts only as long as the pause until another stage comes into being. When the new stage comes into action, then the old teaching becomes sterile and only the organic fragments survive to be embodied in the fresh phase. Even if you were able to hold on to these fragments it would not help you, for the matrix is changed and the relationship between the factors has undergone a subtle rearrangement. Gurdjieff had certain things to say and he said them. The moment that the fragments he had were directed to another sphere, then his teaching ceased to have any value. What exists in the west, based on what he did and said and not on what he knew, is a shadow of subjective imagination. It has become a way of existence rather than a path towards something.'

'Can one,' I asked, 'have profited from following this teaching?'

'Only to the extent that it gave you encouragement to seek some higher consciousness and reminded you that there did exist another realm of existence. As for helping you to attain this realm, it was incapable.'

'If it was pure allegory,' I questioned, 'is it useful to search for the explanations?'

'You do not strike me as being totally devoid of intelligence,' came the withering reply, 'yet your questions show a curious immaturity of thought.

'What inspires you to sift through an outmoded teaching? Suppose, for instance, you discover that the Old Man in *All and Everything* is in fact the Prophet Muhammed, and his grandson Hussein represents Imam Hussein, grandson of Muhammed. Where does that get you? Would it not be better to start by knowing these facts and use them to guide you, rather than using time and energy to plough through things to discover them and then be unable to use them within the context of the earlier activities of Gurdjieff?

'Would you also like to know that the organ Kundabuffer referred to by Gurdjieff is composed of two Persian words *kund,* to blunt, and *farr,* pomp or splendour, the combined word thus being a technical term meaning to blunt the perception by pompousness or self-love? How long would it have taken to work this out and to understand what it means and how it applies? You want to forget the allegories and the intricacies that were relevant before and apply yourself carefully to the main line of the tradition as it is now available to you. You have no time to waste on academic research or intellectual evaluation of half-truths. Worry about the analogy of this, that and the other thing, and you will be feeding your own neuroses. If that is what satisfies you, then follow it and may you retain hold of your sanity.

'My own master, Dil Bar Khan Hululi, taught Gurdjieff. I know what he taught him. Do you wish that I should teach you something that you can no longer apply? Or would you choose a developmental path that is organically in tune with a developing cosmos in which man must find a realisation of himself? Both paths are open to you, but only one can you follow. I will send you to Peshawar if you are ready to go, and from there onwards you will travel alone.'

'Sheikh,' I replied, 'I am ready to travel to Peshawar. My sole intention is to expose myself to a teaching in the hope that, with its help, I may be able to pull myself out of the mire and develop myself. I set out first to follow the path of Gurdjieff knowing no other, but I am ready to follow the path that will give me hope of consciousness.'

'Very well,' answered the Sheikh. 'See Ahmad Mustafa the Smith in Peshawar. Tell him you came to salute the Sheikh ul Mashaikh and he will advise you. Remember that the path will be hard, and if you falter only you can save yourself. Expect no miracles but know that at the end lies deep, permanent consciousness. Ishk Bashad!'

I knew I was right. I had more than a feeling that I had found my way to the source. Perhaps it was that I was already thinking in a fresh way, without filtering everything through a mass of conditioned response. I was no longer, I realised, analysing my motives and remembering myself just for the sake of doing it. I was taking in knowledge and information and consciously storing it up for use when I needed to refer to it. Some of it, I knew, was already working on me and chasing away the cobwebs of a lifetime's developmental indolence.

It was becoming clearer and clearer to me not only that the answers to the questions I sought were present in the Sufi teachings, but that they were much more simply understood when looked at from a new, unconditioned viewpoint. I began to see that it was we who had complicated our lives and clouded over our existing consciousness by introducing factors which had no real place and were only reflections of a state of mind based on a lack of disciplined thinking.

To sink myself completely in the teaching, I knew, was the only way. I could not maintain a flirtatious relationship with it, nor could I become an 'intellectual Sufi', for there are none. It is either complete submission and complete identification with one's teacher or nothing. Half-hearted allegiance could produce only the faintest shadow of what the relationship could be.

Man has always claimed 'intellectual freedom', meaning the right to defect at any time from anything in which he has a diminishing interest in favour of something more exciting. Men's loyalties are shallow even when their own futures are concerned.

It was quite clear to me that academic or intellectual thinking towards a depth teaching such as Sufism was destructive to the person's capacity to learn. Academic or intellectual examination cannot transcend dimension save in its most theoretical form.

Ahmad Mustafa Sarmouni

CHAPTER XIV

AHMAD MUSTAFA SARMOUNI

AHMAD MUSTAFA THE Smith was a man whose age could have been anything over eighty but with a physique of a man of fifty. His face was lined but in repose, and his untroubled gaze gave hint of inner peace. He greeted me gravely in good English though he spoke slowly, measuring his words before he spoke.

Did I, he asked, understand what had motivated my search?

I replied that I was beginning to. At first it had been a search for certain men, but now it was a search for a teaching to fulfil an inner need.

He nodded gravely. 'To follow the teaching of a man is permissible only if it leads to the linking up with the main stream of a valid, developing tradition. Short of this it becomes a cult of personality, and one whose developmental possibilities are severely limited by the achievements of the man one is following.

'Gurdjieff, who stayed in this very house, taught that there existed progress through new thought and action. Since he was himself limited, he could only teach within his limitations and his mandate. Coupled with the time element, you can see that his phase of teaching falls very short of anything complete.

'The man who accepted Gurdjieff into the teaching
was my own master the Sheikh ul Mashaikh. The Sheikh
had chosen him to test out certain of the reactions in the
west to the introduction of Sufi thought that had been
taking place over the centuries. Gurdjieff reported back
regularly on the experiments that he was set to perform.
Even before his death the phase was over, yet some still
drag out what they consider to be the teaching even
though they know little of the technique and even less the
aim. Even if that phase were still valid, they would be
incapable of action. Time and again their right and fitness
to teach have been denied. It is not for us to issue a public
disclaimer denying association with them, though they
speak mysteriously of "centres" and "contacts" and
"monasteries" and what have you. Those who follow and
accept this circus are satisfied with its character and the
promise that it is supposed to hold.'

As he paused I questioned, 'But, sir, is it not somewhat
unfair to those who have reposed their trust in the teaching?'

He gestured irritably. 'Not so, for the real teaching has
ever been available and there for them to find. If they
find an echo in the spurious caperings they indulge in,
then that is their level. Those not dazzled by the outward
show of mystery and exclusiveness and the claim to direct
connection with us have always found a way to make contact with the true teaching. A person can always find us—
witness yourself—but as to whether he is accepted or not
is another question. Do not talk in terms of fair and unfair. You do not know; you are conditioned and subject-

ive. You are not real. You pride yourself on freedom of choice.

'Let me tell you that this very freedom is one of the factors that most confuse and undermine you. It gives you full play for your neuroses, your surface reactions and your aberrations. What you should aim for is freedom *from* choice! Faced with two possibilities, you spend time and effort to decide which to accept. You review the whole spectrum of political, emotional, social, physical, psychological and physiological conditioning before coming up with the answer which, more often than not, does not even satisfy you then. Do you know, can you comprehend, what freedom it gives you if you have *no* choice? Do you know what it means to be able to choose so swiftly and surely that to all intents and purposes you *have* no choice? The choice that you make, your decision, is based on such positive knowledge that the second alternative may as well not exist.

'You will study this book, which is in English,' he went on. 'Some of it will be familiar to you. Do not be surprised, for Gurdjieff drew from it deeply. When the time is right I will send you onwards. You will give as your motive for travel archaeological study, and mention to none your connection with the tradition, save to those who make you this sign or use the password which will be given to you. Have nothing to do with the political currents that ebb and flow in Peshawar. You are a man of letters with no political involvements.'

I remained in Peshawar for a month. During that time I read and re-read *The Walled Garden of Truth* of Hakin Sanai. It was a revelation. There it was, chapter and verse, the basis of Gurdjieff's writings. If I had needed any other proof, this was it.

One evening the summons came. 'Take the mail bus to Jelalabad. Stay at the hotel and await instructions. Your guide will greet you with . . .'

I hardly noticed the dust, the shaking and the discomfort of the journey, so intent was I on preparing myself for the experience I hoped for.

The Sheikh ul Mashaikh

CHAPTER XV

THE SHEIKH UL MASHAIKH

IN JELALABAD I wandered little. The dusty city, despite its gardens and interesting bazaar, held no real interest for me as I was afraid of being out of the hotel if the summons came. It came in an unusual way; I had taken a taxi and directed the driver to the tomb of Amir Habibullah Khan. He drove deep into the old city, stopped outside a small mosque, alighted, opened my door and with a murmured . . . . . led me into the mosque.

In the courtyard, dressed in a white robe and black turban, sat a youngish man with a pointed imperial beard flecked with grey. He motioned me to sit and looked at me reflectively for some seconds before he spoke in perfect English.

'You have come here to find the source of the teaching. You have come to be considered as a pupil. The power houses are not a hundred miles from here but you cannot visit them.'

He fell silent and a feeling of despondency swept over me, but he was speaking again.

'You are a European. You must live, work, study and develop in the west. For this very reason there are centres of activity in the west. You have made this journey, a journey of discovery, to find out where the teaching is and where it can be followed. The teaching is here but you cannot follow it here. You will return to Europe and join a group there. Your journey has consumed much of your time and money, you could have spent both better, but be that as it may.

'You can become a pupil. You can follow the path. You will be under the absolute tutelage of those charged with the direction of this time-phase of the tradition. Let your former self, conditioned and stained by years of avid self-indulgence, fall into the abyss. Work to produce a new surface upon which can be written reality. Question nothing, obey all. Feel your way with your new hands and let your new eyes look outwards to the new horizons. You have spent long, far too long, in devotedly honing a fine edge to your self-esteem. Eschew these meaningless pastimes and live, not just exist.

'Return, then, to Europe, to a place where I will send you. Speak to no one as to where it is or whom you see there, but immerse yourself in its baraka.'

Conclusion

CONCLUSION

I RETURNED TO Europe and sought out the centre to which I had been sent. It was ten miles from my home! I am studying and learning and experiencing at a pace that I could not conceive before. I can write no more nor give more details, for fear that the self-indulgent, the sensation-seekers and the cranks will descend to make a cause out of this 'new order' and disturb the developmental pattern of greatness that I now know it to represent. Others may tread the same path as mine or try to follow the clues as I did, but before they sally forth into the 'mysterious east' let them read a passage from the traditions that I have been allowed to reproduce here:

The Parable of the Loaf or The Three Domains.

Those who have been confused—and many people have undeniably been confused—by the seeming coming and going of phases of teaching about the destiny of man and the 'inner life' should first listen to this ancient parable.

Let us consider, as we unfold the parable, three things; the wheat in the fields, the water in the stream and the salt in the mine. This is the condition of natural man, the state of the First Domain. The three items are in a state of potentiality. Each has grown up, moved or developed in its own way.

In the Second Domain, however, we have a state in which something further can be done. The wheat is ground into flour, the water is collected and stored, the salt extracted and refined. This is a Domain of activity, of labour and of the application of certain expert knowledge to the production of certain results. This is the phase of the theoretical teacher, too, in which certain materials are shaped for the coming of the Third Domain.

The Third Domain comes into being after the water and salt are mixed with the flour to make dough. When the yeast is brought from a source, and the oven made ready for the baking of a loaf, the necessary knowledge for making bread is brought as well. This depends as much upon 'touch' as upon theoretical knowledge.

This is the stage of what we call a School.

In the stage of the raw materials being available but not worked upon, they can have only the effect which is natural to them. Something is done—but only in its own Domain—the first. In the Second Domain, when the materials are being discovered, processed, systematised and preserved, it is folly to try to work upon the Third Domain's concerns. It is only in the Third Domain that the final processes come about, which demand the appearance of a specialist 'baker'.

The present situation is that of the Third Domain. People who are attached to the First and Second Domains are not able to see the process clearly. Hence most of their questions are asked from a basis of the assumption that they are in the first two Domains. Others are working in the Second Domain, without realising that the bread is about to be baked. Until this concept of the ordered and orderly progress of the Great Work is clearly accepted, confusion will continue, and it will not be possible to communicate with the people whose incoherence is partly due to the confusion of the Domains and partly to their desire to attach themselves to something without allowing themselves to become aware of the very real stages of The Work.

Nothing is done by experimentation, by trial and error. Neither is anything done by repetitiously sticking to the work of a Domain which is not of this time, or this place, or this community and its real necessities. Its real necessities differ from the generalised theoretical necessities of mankind as a whole, as delineated in preliminary material which is being used by many people as real 'Work' material.

The success of the Work of the Third Domain always depends on the right formulation, at the right time, in the right place, with the right people. This is the affirmation of the permanent custodians of the Tradition.

What I had sought so long I have finally found. Not in the grotesque caperings of an outdated system, not in the dialogues of the intellectuals, nor, for that matter, in the deep and mysterious recesses of the Hindu Kush, but right here in my own country. I have found that the real Tradition, true to its purpose and its mandate, has spread to encompass mankind and to offer the only real, deep and purposeful Path that can lead man to a realisation of his destiny.

Index

INDEX